Praise for Amy James's Knowledge Essentials S[...]

"Knowledge Essentials is a remarkable series that will benefit children of all abilities and learning styles. Amy James has taken a close look at curriculum standards and testing around the country and developed simple and creative activities that support what's being taught at each grade level, while remaining sensitive to the fact that children learn at different rates and in different ways. I highly recommend it for all parents who want to make a difference in their children's education."

—Michael Gurian, author of *Boys and Girls Learn Differently*
and *The Wonder of Boys*

"Finally, a book about teaching young children by somebody who knows her stuff! I can (and will) wholeheartedly recommend this series to the ever-growing number of parents who ask me for advice about how they can help their children succeed in elementary school."

—LouAnne Johnson, author of *Dangerous Minds*
and *The Queen of Education*

"Having examined state standards nationwide, Amy James has created innovative and unique games and exercises to help children absorb what they have to learn, in ways that will help them want to learn. Individualized to the child's own learning style, this is a must-have series for parents who want to maximize their child's ability to succeed in and out of the classroom."

—Myrna B. Shure, Ph.D., author of *Thinking Parents, Thinking Child*

"The books in Amy James's timely and unique Knowledge Essentials series give parents a clear idea of what their children are learning and provide the tools they need to help their children live up to their full academic potential. This is must reading for any parent with a school-age child."

—Michele Borba, Ed.D., author of *Nobody Likes Me,*
Everybody Hates Me and *No More Misbehavin'*

Published by Jossey-Bass
A Wiley Imprint
989 Market Street, San Francisco, CA 94103-1741—www.josseybass.com

Readers should be aware that Internet Web sites offered as citations and/or sources for further information may have changed or disappeared between the time this was written and when it is read.

Limit of Liability/Disclaimer of Warranty: While the publisher and author have used their best efforts in preparing this book, they make no representations or warranties with respect to the accuracy or completeness of the contents of this book and specifically disclaim any implied warranties of merchantability or fitness for a particular purpose. No warranty may be created or extended by sales representatives or written sales materials. The advice and strategies contained herein may not be suitable for your situation. You should consult with a professional where appropriate. Neither the publisher nor author shall be liable for any loss of profit or any other commercial damages, including but not limited to special, incidental, consequential, or other damages.

Jossey-Bass books and products are available through most bookstores. To contact Jossey-Bass directly, call our Customer Care Department within the U.S. at 800-956-7739, outside the U.S. at 317-572-3986, or fax 317-572-4002.

Jossey-Bass also publishes its books in a variety of electronic formats. Some content that appears in print may not be available in electronic books.

Library of Congress Cataloging-in-Publication Data has been applied for.

ISBN: 978-0-471-74815-1

Printed in the United States of America
PB Printing 10 9 8 7 6 5 4 3 2 1

JB JOSSEY-BASS

SCHOOL SUCCESS FOR CHILDREN WITH SPECIAL NEEDS

Everything You Need to Know to Help Your Child Learn

AMY JAMES

BICENTENNIAL

1807

WILEY

2007

BICENTENNIAL

John Wiley & Sons, Inc.

In loving memory of my dad, E. W. James,
and
my stepdad, Jim King

CONTENTS

Introduction   xi

PART I   Know Your Rights   1

1   Determining Eligibility   3

Step 1: The Categorical Element   5
Step 2: The Functional Element   6
Evaluating Children Under Age Three   10
Evaluating Children Ages Three to Twenty-One   11
Eligibility   13
What's Next   15

2   Individual Family Services Plan   17

What Are Early Intervention Services?   17
Preparing to Write the Individual Family Services Plan   21
Transitioning from the Individual Family Services Plan to the Individual Education Plan   25

3 Individual Education Plan 27

What Are Special-Education Services? 27
Preparing to Write the Individual Education Plan 29
The IEP 32
What's Next 37

4 Procedural Due Process 39

What If You and the School Disagree? 39
Is It Possible to Win a Due-Process Hearing? 44

PART II The Special-Needs Classroom 47

5 The Regular Classroom Versus the Special-Needs Classroom 49

When Your Child Should Be in a Special-Needs Classroom 49
When to Include Your Child in the Regular Classroom 51
Tips for Buying Educational Products or Toys for Your Special-Needs
 Child 57

6 Accommodations and Modifications 61

Preschool 63
Elementary School 64
Middle School and High School 69

7 Administration 73

Meetings 75
Paperwork 76

PART III   Special-Needs Tips by Grade Level   81

8   Preschool to Kindergarten   83

Building-Block Skills   84
Reading Readiness   86
Writing Readiness   89
Math Readiness   91
Assessment   94

9   Elementary School   99

Building-Block Skills   99
Reading Skills   103
Writing Skills   108
Math Skills   113
Assessment   119

10   Middle School   123

Transitioning from Elementary School to Middle School   123
Building-Block Skills   124
Assessment   139

11   High School   143

Compensation Strategies   143
Self-Regulation and Compensation Strategies   145
Time-Management Skills   147
Life Skills   148

12 **Exiting Special Services   149**

Transitioning from High School to the Real World   149

Choosing Colleges for Students with Disabilities   155

How Can You Help Your Child Be Successful in College?   157

Preparing for Postsecondary Education   163

Appendix A: Acronyms   167

Appendix B: The Forms   197

Appendix C: IEP Sample Form   225

Appendix D: Glossary   237

Appendix E: Disability Checklists by Age   243

Appendix F: Internet Resources   259

References   265

Index   279

INTRODUCTION

One day you are a carefree parent on the move, and the next day you are the parent of a child with special needs. If your child is physically disabled, the next day may have been the first day your child entered the world. Other parents are unaware of the disability until they see their child's development or lack of it. Either way, your life as a parent is dramatically different from what you had expected. Your life and your child's are intertwined, and you are realizing that in order to protect your child's rights and your own rights, you must be intimately aware of the services available for your child's special needs and the legislation that regulates those services.

As a parent of a special-needs child, you will spend a lot of time ensuring that you and your child receive the services necessary to level the playing field for your child with the other kids. Whether your child needs glasses to see normally, needs assistive devices to interact with and move about in the community, or needs to learn mechanisms that will assist her in emotionally or developmentally perceiving the world as others do, your goal as a parent is to ensure that your child and your family receive the assistance that you have the right to receive.

If your child is severely disabled, you already have been introduced to public and private services that can assist you with the responsibilities associated with raising a special-needs child. If your child is moderately disabled or demonstrates developmental delays, your pediatrician may have recommended that your child be evaluated for early intervention services provided by the government. Now that your child is in school, you must manage the environment in which your child is learning, how he learns, the learning services he needs, and social environments. Every aspect of it can be confusing, but this book will help you understand the basics of your new world, starting with the most important question: Does your child have special needs?

There are two pieces of legislation that determine whether your child has needs that require special accommodations under the law. Under Section 504 of the Vocational Rehabilitation Act of 1973, no student with a physical or mental impairment that substantially limits one or more major life activities, or who has a record of such an impairment, or who is regarded as having such an impairment, shall solely by reason of this impairment "be excluded from participation in, be denied the benefits of, or be subjected to discrimination." This language was in line with the many pieces of antidiscrimination legislation considered or passed during the 1960s and 1970s. It meant that students with disabilities could no longer be excluded from the regular classroom or regular activities at school just because of a disability. The Act was written in broad language, and schools needed help implementing the legislation consistently from year to year and from town to town. The same legislation was revised several times under the name Individuals with Disabilities Act (IDEA), with the intent of ensuring that individuals with disabilities receive the appropriate services to help them learn. IDEA is reauthorized on a regular basis (most recently in 2004 and it took effect on July 1, 2005) with revisions, and the current version will be reauthorized in 2011. Students receiving accommodations under Sec. 504—the 1975 version is still in effect—are eligible for the same range of accommodations as students with disabilities under IDEA/s.115.76.

Although all students with disabilities under IDEA/s.115.76 also meet the criteria for protection under Sec. 504, there are a *limited* number of students who are not considered students with disabilities under IDEA/s.115.76, but who do meet the criteria for protection under Sec. 504. Examples of these situations include students with health conditions (such as diabetes or asthma) or mobility impairment (such as paraplegia) who have an impairment that substantially limits one or more major life activities, but who are determined not to need special education services in accordance with IDEA. Students qualifying only under Sec. 504 criteria are entitled to accommodations and services necessary to benefit from all educational activities available to other students, including state (and district) assessment activities. For these students, appropriate accommodations and services must be documented in an Individualized Accommodation Plan (IAP), including any accommodations necessary for participation in assessment activities.

Just to add another law to the mix, the No Child Left Behind Act (NCLB) requires that all students, including those with disabilities, meet their states' definition of academic proficiency by the 2013–2014 school year. The reauthorized IDEA specifies that alternate assessment is to be provided for the small number of students with disabilities for whom the standardized assessment is inappropriate even with accommodations. NCLB also requires that teachers be subject area experts and demonstrate that through special certifications. A special-needs teacher often teaches multiple subjects to multiple ages during a single day, so NCLB may drastically change the way your child's school is providing services that meet the requirements of IDEA.

School Success for Students with Special Needs is your resource for everything from understanding the legislation that governs the requirements and services associated with being disabled to laying out these important areas, grade-by-grade and age-by-age:

- Does my child have a physical, learning, or emotional disability?

- How do schools and teachers accommodate children with disabilities at different ages and in different grades?

- How can I help my child be successful at school?
- What kind of paperwork am I going to be dealing with?

Special education may sound a little ominous, especially if you're thinking of the classroom at the end of the hallway that you hardly ever went near. If you are, that means you are thinking of special education as a place, a classroom, or a part of the school that is sectioned off for the "other kids." It isn't a place. Special education is a service, and it's an important service that your child may need.

Many people often do not understand what special education is and the tremendous benefits in providing a proper education to children with special needs. Congress recognized that for the first time in 1975, when it enacted the Individuals with Disabilities Education Act (IDEA), then known as the Education of All Handicapped Students Act, or Public Law (PL) 94–142. The law has been revised more than once, but we will be focusing on the law as it stands today, based on the 2004 revision that became law effective July 1, 2005.

The basic components of IDEA are important because the rest of the legislation stems from their principles. Let's take a look at some of them:

1. *Zero reject.* A rule against excluding any student. This is how it should be, right?

2. *Nondiscriminatory evaluation.* Schools are required to evaluate students fairly to determine whether they have a disability and, if so, what kind and how extensive. The principle ensures that students' disabilities are not ignored or that disabilities are not purposely found where there are none.

3. *Appropriate education.* Schools must provide individually tailored education for each student based on the evaluation and augmented by related services and supplementary aids and services.

An important component of IDEA, an individually tailored appropriate education, is documented and achieved through something called an individual education plan (IEP). We will be talking a lot about IEPs throughout this book.

4. *Least restrictive environment.* This is important: schools must educate students with disabilities together with nondisabled students to the maximum extent possible for the students with disabilities.

   The concept of *least restrictive environment* is what prevents students with disabilities from being put away in one part of the school, or in a school by themselves, and not being allowed to learn and interact with students that do not have disabilities. Needless to say, there are times when students with special needs benefit from being in an environment comprised solely of other children like themselves. There are also times in which a teacher in a "regular" classroom cannot best serve the disabled student's needs. Permanently separating the two groups of students is never appropriate and that is what the concept of least restrictive environment prevents. Least restrictive environments prevent students from being kept in institutions, unless that is the only way that they can be served. Least restrictive environments can be thought of as a continuum, such as the following:

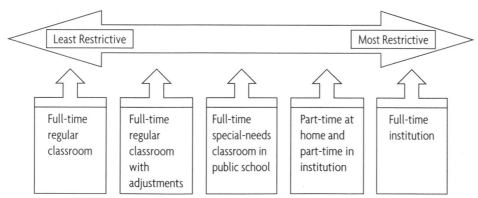

Figure I.1. Environment Continuum

There are many points in between, but this gives you the general idea.

5. *Procedural due process.* Schools must provide due process with respect to a school's actions, including a right to sue in court.

    Procedural due process is a hard concept. It is basically the right to be heard about an issue through procedures, or in an orderly manner that tries to be fair to all sides. We'll delve into this more in Chapter Four.

6. *Parent and student participation.* Schools must collaborate with parents and adolescent students in designing and carrying out special education programs.

    You, the parent, are a respected and valuable component of your child's education.

Those are the basic principles of IDEA, and they will be important in understanding the more detailed components of the legislation. The rest of the book will help you marry these principles with their daily implementation.

A word before we continue: the first few chapters in this book are denser than the rest of the book because they describe complicated legislation and some tricky forms. If you already know your child has special needs, you may want to start with these chapters. If you only suspect that your child has special needs, you may want to start with the grade-level overviews or refer to the grade-level checklists in Appendix E.

Know Your Rights 1

Although all students with disabilities under IDEA/s.115.76 also meet the criteria for protection under Sec. 504, a *limited* number of students are not considered students with disabilities under IDEA/ s.115.76 but *do* meet the criteria for protection under Sec. 504. Examples of these situations include students with health conditions (for example, diabetes or asthma) or a mobility impairment (for example, paraplegia) who have an impairment that substantially limits one or more major life activities but who are determined not to need special-education services in accordance with the Individuals with Disabilities Education Act (IDEA).

Students qualifying only under Sec. 504 criteria are entitled to the accommodations and services necessary for them to benefit from all educational activities available to other students, including state (and district) assessment activities. For these students, appropriate accommodations and services must be documented in an Individualized Accommodation Plan (IAP), including any accommodations necessary for participation in assessment activities.

IDEA is designed to ensure that children and young adults with disabilities receive the educational services that are best for them. So, as you would expect, there are some eligibility requirements. Let's take a look at the basic requirements of IDEA (Table 1.1).

Table 1.1.   Basic Requirements of the Individuals with Disabilities Education Act (IDEA)

Component	Legal Requirements	In Other Words
Eligibility based on need	IDEA defines special education as specifically designed instruction, at no cost to the child's parents, to meet the unique needs of a student with a disability (20 U.S.C., §1401[3]).	Special education is for children whose needs cannot be met in a regular classroom.
Where special education is provided	Special education occurs in the classroom, student's home, hospitals and institutions, and other settings.	Wherever there are students with special-education needs.
Components of special education	To meet a student's needs, it is usually necessary to provide more than individualized instruction by supplementing instruction with "related services," namely, the services that are necessary to assist the student to benefit from special education (20 U.S.C., §1401[22]).	If a student needs special services, they will be provided. There is a list of special services in Chapter Seven.
Category and function of special needs to be eligible for special needs	There is a two-part standard for eligibility: (1) the categorical element—the student must have a disability; and (2) the functional element—the disability must cause the student to need specially designed instruction.	A student is eligible for special education and related services if the student has a disability and, because of the disability, needs specially designed instruction.

Step 1: The Categorical Element

To meet the categorical element of IDEA eligibility, the legislation defines the categories of disabilities it serves. They are defined in Table 1.2.

Table 1.2.   Categories of Disabilities for Children Ages Six Through Twenty-One

Specific Learning Disabilities	Definition
Emotional disturbance	A mood disorder; an affective disorder in which the person tends to respond excessively and sometimes violently.
Mental retardation	Subnormal intellectual development as a result of congenital causes, brain injury, or disease and characterized by any of various cognitive deficiencies, including impaired learning, social, and vocational ability. Also called *mental disability*.
Multiple disabilities	A person that has more than one disability.
Deaf-blindness	A person with little or no useful sight and hearing.
Autism	A neurodevelopmental disorder characterized by markedly abnormal social interaction, communication ability, patterns of interests, and patterns of behavior.
Other health impairments	Other health issues that affect a person's ability to learn and his or her social or vocational abilities.
Orthopedic requirements	A disorder of the muscles or bones that requires an assistive device(s) to enable the person to function in part or completely.
Traumatic brain injury	Also called acquired brain injury, intracranial injury, or simply head injury; occurs when a sudden trauma causes damage to the brain. Symptoms of a TBI can be mild, moderate, or severe, depending on the extent of the damage to the brain. Outcome can be anything from complete recovery to permanent disability.
Speech or language impairments	A type of communication disorder in which "normal" speech is disrupted. This can mean stuttering, lisps, vocal dysphonia, and so on.
Hearing impairments	Little to no useful hearing ability.
Visual impairments	Little to no useful seeing ability.

The same categories apply to children starting at age three, but for children ages three through nine, the state may also give special education to children that meet only the functional requirement. This is very important to remember: IDEA states that kids ages three through nine can receive special services for learning problems that fall outside of the scope of the defined disabilities. These children are eligible for services if they are experiencing developmental delays in the following areas:

- *Physical development:* such as a physical disability that is diagnosed by a physician.
- *Cognitive development:* characterized by many factors that are listed in the developmental checklists found in Appendix E.
- *Communication development:* isn't speaking clearly or is displaying an obvious speech disorder such as a lisp.
- *Social development:* these are usually characterized by behavioral problems and/or impulse control.
- *Emotional development:* this often goes hand-in-hand with social development and has many of the same indicators: behavioral problems or impulse control.

Step 2: The Functional Element

The primary component of the functional element of eligibility for special education is that your child demonstrates a need for special education. In other words, your child's disability or delay causes him to need specially designed instruction.

The evaluation activities and procedures that your child will take part in are used to determine:

- Whether your child has a disability that adversely affects educational performance

- Whether your child requires special education and any necessary related services

- Whether your child requires supplementary aids or services

- The nature and extent of special education, related services, or supplementary aids and services that your child needs

The functional requirement sounds subjective, but there are many ways to tell whether a child will benefit from special instruction. Your local school district will evaluate your child in all areas related to the suspected disability in order to identify what special education and related services are needs. The areas of evaluation should include, if appropriate:

- Health

- Vision

- Hearing

- Social skills

- Emotional status

- General intelligence

- Academic performance

- Communication skills

- Motor abilities

Evaluation activities include the following:

- Determining your child's eligibility and need for special education and related services

- Measuring your child's present levels of functioning, needs, abilities, and limitations

- Drawing conclusions about the significance of findings as they relate to the general education curriculum and instructional programming

- Providing information that will assist the Individual Education Plan (IEP) team in making decisions about the special-education program, including necessary related services, assistive technology needs, extended school-year services, and support services

Testing for Disabilities

Each potential disability has an array of tests that help professionals evaluate:

- Whether your child has disabilities
- The extent to which to your child's disabilities exist, and
- How to best assist your child in overcoming her disabilities.

Physical Disabilities

This book is about the educational accommodation of students with special needs. Your child's doctors are the only people qualified to speak to the medical existence, degree, or other status of your child's physical disabilities. The recommendations made by medical professionals must be documented so that your child's school will be required to accommodate them. All services related to physical disabilities will be driven by physician recommendations. If your child's physical disability also entails learning disabilities, those will be diagnosed and assessed through a different array of instruments.

Learning Disabilities

Learning disorders are first *informally flagged* by observing significant delays in your child's skill development. You or your child's teacher or physician may be the first to notice the delays. If your child is in elementary school, a rule of thumb is that a two-grade delay is usually considered significant. If your child is older, a two-year delay is not considered to be significant but a three-year delay is. The *actual diagnosis* of learning disabilities is made by administering standardized tests that compare your child's abilities to what is considered to be a normal score for a child of that age.

I can hear you now: "Well, what are those tests, who gives them, and how do they score the answers?" The answers are as varied as the day is long. There are over three hundred diagnostic tests for learning disabilities. Your school district purchases the tests from the company that they feel is most reliable and with which their school psychometrist is the most familiar. The school district will give you information about the specific tests they use; if they don't, you should ask for it. So, who and what is a school psychometrist? This person is an educator who also has at least a master's degree in psychology and who is in charge of all testing and placement tests, procedures, and implementation of special services in a school district. The psychometrist knows her stuff. She has taught, worked as a psychologist, and been trained to administer and interpret the assessments for every special-needs student in the school district.

Each type of learning disorder is unique, and the tests used to identify each of them and the degrees to which they exist are ordered on a case-by-case basis, like a prescription. That, coupled with the sheer number of tests, makes it impossible to describe each of them, but your school will give you information about them and you should ask as many questions as you feel are necessary to make you feel comfortable with the process. If you do not feel comfortable, you always have the right to pay for an outside evaluation. If that occurs, you will want to have a record of the tests your child has already been given. The categories of assessments are:

1. *Aptitude/cognitive ability.* A complete intellectual assessment with all subtests and standard scores reported is essential.

2. *Academic achievement.* A comprehensive academic achievement battery is essential, with all subtests and standard scores reported

for those subtests administered. The battery must include current levels of academic functioning in relevant areas such as reading (decoding and comprehension), mathematics, and oral and written language.

3. *Information processing.* Specific areas of information processing (for example, short- and long-term memory, sequential memory, auditory and visual perception/processing, processing speed, executive functioning, and motor ability) should be addressed.

Other assessment measures, such as classroom tests and informal assessment procedures or observations, may be helpful in determining performance across a variety of areas and should be a part of your child's diagnostic portfolio. Other formal assessment measures may be integrated with the categories above to help rule in or rule out the learning disability to differentiate it from neurological or psychiatric disorders. In addition to standardized tests, it is also very useful to include informal observations of the student during test administration; your child's behavior during testing can help the school psychometrist adjust for factors such as nervousness or lack of impulse control during testing when analyzing your child's performance.

Evaluating Children Under Age Three

If your child exhibits signs of a disability before age three, you will begin working with an early intervention team. The evaluation for early intervention generally starts with your child's pediatrician, and on referral to the special services coordinator for your area, your child will be evaluated on an individual basis. Your child will be evaluated by other doctors if physical disabilities are suspected, or by other professionals such as those described in the Testing section of this chapter. Your child must be demonstrating developmental delays in a combination of areas (and there is no magic formula here: it could be a severe delay in one area or slight delays in a number of them) such as:

- Health
- Vision
- Hearing
- Social and emotional skills
- Cognitive development
- Motor skills
- Communication skills

Evaluation activities include:

- Determining your child's eligibility and need for early intervention services
- Measuring your child's present levels of functioning, needs, abilities, and limitations
- Drawing conclusions about the significance of findings as they relate to your child's healthy development
- Providing information that will assist the school in making decisions when your child enters school about the special-education program, including necessary related services, assistive technology needs, extended school-year services, and support services

If your child is recommended for evaluation, you will begin working with a special services coordinator. If your child does have a special need, you will begin working with an early intervention team. Table 1.3 explains the differences between the two.

Evaluating Children Ages Three to Twenty-One

The evaluation group will develop the evaluation report that includes:

- The disability that requires special education and related services, if a disability exists

Table 1.3. Assistance Stages

Special Services Coordinator	Early Intervention Team
They are employed by the state health department to meet the requirements of IDEA to serve children that are at risk before they enter the school system in the hopes of improving that child's development. The coordinator is assigned to a geographic region that is based on populations (where it is a county in one area, it may be a portion of a school district in another). The special services coordinator is called into action when your physician recommends your child for further evaluation.	A team that includes your special services coordinator in which you and your family have a lot of input in deciding who becomes a member of the team and how they help your child and your family. When your child is formally diagnosed with a special need, the early intervention team is called in to help determine what services will best serve your child and your family.

- How the disability or disabilities affects your child's involvement and progress in the general curriculum, or for preschool children, in appropriate activities

- Recommendations to the IEP team with respect to special education and related services needed, materials or equipment, instructional and curricular practices, student management strategies, the need for services beyond 180 school days, and location of services

- Any necessary professional judgments and the facts or reasons in support of the judgments

- Special Education or IEP Team (ages three to twenty-one):

    A team of educators, the school psychometrist and other professionals, including you, that is chosen and governed by your local school district. There is no special services coordinator as the school district now coordinates your child's services.

    The special-education building team is responsible for notifying parents of evaluation meetings. The special-education building team

Table 1.4.   Special-Education Teams

Special-Education Evaluation Team a.k.a. the Individual Education Plan (IEP) Team	Special-Education Building Team
When your child enters school with a disability or is diagnosed with a disability through the school system, you will be working with the evaluation team, more often called the IEP team, to determine what the test scores mean, if additional tests are needed, what special services your child may need in the regular classroom, and how much of his day he may be spending in a special-education classroom.	The special-education building team implements and documents all of the special services that are provided by the school. Diagnostic testing is coordinated by the IEP team and is administered by the school district; special services that are delivered through the building are coordinated by the building team. The building team is comprised of the regular classroom teacher (if your child spends part of her time in a regular classroom), the special-education teacher, a school counselor, and a building administrator. The special-education teacher is generally the team leader.

is not an evaluation team (even though they will be a part of it), but should be considered to be more of an implementation team. Parents will be provided with a copy of the report on completion, and the special-education building team will implement it.

Eligibility

The evaluation group and the parent will determine whether the student is a special-education student. You will be provided with a copy of the evaluation report and the documentation of determination of eligibility.

Children Who Are Not Eligible

- Your child is not eligible if the determinant factor is a lack of instruction in English or limited English proficiency.
- Your child is not eligible when the determinant factor is a lack of instruction in reading or mathematics.

Children Who Are Eligible

Eligible children remain eligible for special-education services until one of three events occurs:

1. A reevaluation determines that your child no longer needs special-education services.

2. Your child meets the district's high school graduation requirements (and some schools are required to develop procedures for granting high school graduation credits for students with disabilities), or

3. Your child reaches age twenty-one. However, if your child's twenty-first birthday occurs after August 31, he continues to be eligible for special education and any necessary related services for the remainder of the school year.

Independent Educational Evaluations

If in this process you have been in legitimate (or illegitimate) disagreement with the evaluation or reevaluation of your child, you have the right to request an independent educational evaluation (IEE) at the school's expense. There will be some criteria for the outside evaluator to meet, such as that he must be

- Licensed, credentialed, or otherwise qualified in your state of residence to practice and to perform an evaluation in the specific professional discipline for which an IEE is sought

- Knowledgeable and experienced in evaluating children with similar disabilities

- Geographically located within your state, and

- Available to the district at a maximum fee that does not overly exceed the prevailing average for similar evaluations. This means that if the average fee in your area is $70 per hour, this is what the school district is required to pay.

What's Next?

The evaluation process is complete and your child needs special-education services. Now what happens? The chapters that follow will tell you about the next stage in the process. If your child is under the age of three, you will receive an Individual Family Services Plan (IFSP), which is described in Chapter Two. If your child is age three or older, your child will receive an Individual Education Plan, which is described in Chapter Three. The next three chapters address the types of disabilities that you can receive services for: physical disabilities, learning disabilities, and behavior/social disabilities.

Individual Family Services Plan

2

IDEA states that children under the age of three need to be considered separately from children age three and older. Children under age three have different educational needs than older children do. Younger children need Early Intervention services to try to close the gap in developmental and physical abilities as quickly as possible.

Early Intervention services are services that are offered by the state and local governments to meet the portion of IDEA that serves children under the age of three. Each state calls them Early Intervention services, and they are made available through the Department of Health.

What Are Early Intervention Services?

Early Intervention is an integrated developmental service available to the families of children, between birth and three years of age, for whom there are developmental concerns due to identified disabilities, or whose typical development is at risk due to certain birth or environmental circumstances.

Your state health department is responsible for administering and overseeing the system of Early Intervention services, for certifying programs and monitoring activities. The state designates appropriate community-based programs to serve all cities and towns in your area.

To properly provide services to each child based on that child's needs, the federal government requires that the local service providers create an Individual Family Services Plan (IFSP). This is an important plan that documents what services your child needs in order to learn and develop. The IFSP is developed in a partnership among:

- *You:* you are the most knowledgeable about the needs of your child and family
- *Early Intervention staff:* professionals such as educators, psychologists, or medical professionals
- *Others:* anyone you may want to include in the development of this plan such as a grandparent who often cares for your child

The Early Intervention staff work in partnership with people who are present in your child's natural environment, which may include settings other than your home. Individual team members may include speech, occupational and physical therapists, developmental educators, social workers, psychologists, and nurses. In addition, Early Intervention programs may work with consultants in areas such as nutrition, adaptive equipment, and behavior management.

Together, you develop the plan that includes the goals and services that will best serve your child and your family. The IFSP is updated at least once a year and reviewed every six months. Additions and changes can be made anytime you and the providers agree it is necessary.

How Does My Child Get Identified for Early Intervention Services?

Referrals to Early Intervention programs are an open process and are made directly to the individual program. In other words, if you or your doctor want a service for your child, all you have to do is ask for it and your child will be evaluated for eligibility. Referrals may be made by any person concerned about a child's development and are often made by family members, physicians, hospitals, community social-service agencies, and family friends. Families are encouraged to refer themselves, but if referred by someone else, you will be contacted to request permission to proceed. If you decide to proceed, an evaluation/assessment will take place and, if eligibility is established and the family elects to receive services, an IFSP will be developed by the team in which the family is a member. Programs include speech therapy, physical therapy, occupational therapy, vision therapy, transportation, psychological assistance, and more.

The following is a list of information to supply to the program at the time of referral or the acceptance of the referral:

Child's name

Your name

Address

Telephone numbers (work and home)

Child's date of birth

Primary pediatrician

Other physicians/agencies/services involved

Reason for referral

Child's insurance coverage

Your Child Has Been Identified for Early Intervention Services

What Is Your Role?

Once your child has been identified for Early Intervention services, it's important for you to understand your responsibilities and what you can do for your child. No one knows your child as well as you do.

You will likely be the primary person when implementing the IFSP, so you want to be an important part of the planning. You need to participate in every part of the process to ensure that you achieve a goal that most benefits your child and your family. You may want to think about some things as this gets started:

- What are some of the things you and your child do every day?
- What activities does your child enjoy doing?
- What do you need right now to support you as a family?
- What do your children without disabilities need to feel important?
- What are your hopes and dreams for your child?
- What are your and your child's limitations?

What Is the Role of Early Intervention Services?

Early Intervention is responsible for seeing that your family receives the available services that will best help your child. The services are broad and they are designed to be delivered based on your child's needs, so first a services coordinator is assigned to work with you throughout the process. The services coordinator is paid by the state to help your family find resources and support that will benefit your child. The coordinator will work with you up until your child reaches the age of three, or sooner if the family no longer needs the service. She will work with you to put together a team of people who can make diagnoses and recommendations for your child's special needs. The services coordinator is responsible for helping your family, but is also responsible for seeing that the program is administered properly.

Everything that Early Intervention does for your child is going to be documented in your IFSP. To make an IFSP, you have to start by setting up the team of people who will help create it.

Preparing to Write the Individual Family Services Plan

There are a few things you will need to do before you write the IFSP that will govern the services your child receives. First, you need to select a team of people to help. You'll need to meet with your team beforehand in order to prepare for the actual IFSP planning meeting. This process is probably more important and can take more effort than the actual meeting where you write the plan, so be prepared!

Forming a Team

Team members are defined by the needs of your child and family. Your family has the primary opportunity to set up the team. You may prefer a small team or you may want everyone involved in your team meetings. The quantity of people on your team doesn't matter as much as the variety of team members. In order to write an effective IFSP, you'll need a lot of different types of information (medical, developmental, psychological, and so forth), so you will need different types of people to collect the information, relay it to you, and prescribe a plan for the highest possible outcomes. It is just as important to consider support people, such as extended family and child-care providers, as it is to consider providers of services when setting up the team. Your team provides insight to your child and her needs, so provide a variety of perspectives of your child so that the most complete picture of your child can be drawn and served.

If some team members cannot be present at a meeting (such as a physician) other creative ways to obtain their input should be explored. It is very important for a variety of people to be at every meeting. It is also important to note that some meetings require certain participants to fulfill rules and regulations to comply with IDEA and it is the responsibility of the services coordinator to make sure that these people are present and that you understand any regulations that apply. IDEA requires that the team members be comprised of individuals that have different areas of expertise and if they are not all present, each of your child's needs may not be addressed.

Preparing for the Meeting

You will work with your services coordinator to prepare for your planning meeting. Sometimes it is helpful to request a meeting with the services coordinator prior to the IFSP meeting, and ask him to inform the team members of the family's goals so everyone can begin thinking of ways and resources that might be helpful in meeting these goals. During this time, the services coordinator can help you understand what will take place at the IFSP meeting and the part each person will play. You can decide to run the meeting or the services coordinator could plan to take that role. It is usually better to let the services coordinator lead the meetings, just to make sure that all bases are covered. Remember, your services coordinator does this for a living and his experience will add a lot to the meeting.

When you are ready for your meeting, you should expect to know:

1. Most of what is going to happen before the meeting. Issues such as evaluation results, the possibility of stopping or starting a service, and anything else should be discussed with everyone prior to the actual meeting. This gives people time to think about issues, gather data, and develop informed opinions about your child prior to documenting or changing the plan.

2. Families, along with team, set the outcomes.

3. The plan will contain achievable steps to meet the outcomes.

4. You can decline a service without fear of not being able to get that service at a later time.

5. Any IFSP plan is a living document. It can and should always be changed and updated, at least once a year, and reviewed every six months.

There are several things to remember during this time, particularly when interacting with the people that make up the team:

- Be yourself.

- Don't be defensive.

- Don't be demanding unless it is your last resort and you are certain that you are the only one who is correct.

During this process you can expect to be asked for information such as:

- How much support you have, especially natural supports such as other family members, your church, neighbors, and your friends

- How your child with the disability changes the family's life

- How your family works and what your values and beliefs are

- What your hopes and dreams are for your child

- What scares you about your child's disability, and

- What your family's priorities are

You will need to be able to list achievable outcomes in your IFSP. You may want to list outcomes such as the ones listed below:

I would like the entire family to learn sign language.

My child will be able to sit up to play with toys.

I need time for myself.

Carrie will imitate new words.

Molly will look at me when she is sitting in her highchair.

We would like to increase feeding by mouth so we can work toward getting Susan off her G-tube.

John will use single words to tell Mom what he wants.

I need to spend more time with my children who do not have special needs.

We would like to find a playgroup that my child can attend with kids her age.

I want Luis to sleep through the night.

Your desired outcomes may be similar or very different. Write them down and be ready to talk about how you think community services may help your family.

Writing the IFSP

It's the day of the planning meeting and you should have already put a fair amount of time and effort into gathering the information and preparing for the day. The truth is that you have already done the hardest and most important parts, which are gathering the diagnosis, seeking services, and listing achievable outcomes. Today is more about the opportunity to have a group conversation for your child's benefit with people who all know him, but may have never directly interacted with him until now. This alone will spark thoughts and ideas about how to help your family.

This day is significant because you will create the document that states what will happen to help your child. It's important to have something in writing that shows the work families and staff will do together. The IFSP should include the following information:

- Your child's basic information, including assessment results, your family's concerns, and your child's strengths
- Outcomes you want to achieve for your child and family
- The strategies and methods to achieve the plan
- Services your child will receive: how often, by whom, when, and where
- The name of your services coordinator; it may be listed as something else, but this is the person who helps develop your plan,

ensures that it is carried out, and makes sure that you receive your rights and procedural safeguards

- The names of all of your team members, their roles, and their contact information
- Next steps, including when the team will meet again and how to transition from Early Intervention services (if appropriate)

The IFSP will be written on a standard form used by your state that should include all of the information you need. You can find a sample form in Appendix B.

Transitioning from the Individual Family Services Plan to the Individual Education Plan

Your child will only be served by Early Intervention services until age three. At that time, if your child continues to require special services, you will transition to a special-education committee run by your local school district. As your child approaches age three, your Early Intervention team will begin writing transition activities into your IFSP that will help your child and your family move on to the Individual Education Plan (IEP). They will include such things as an evaluation and recommendation for services, the planned date of your first meeting with the local school district, plans for your child to stay in the same preschool, and other activities, if appropriate and possible.

The biggest differences between the two systems are as follows:

- No service coordinator is provided by the school district. The school district works with you to become responsible for any preschool special-education needs of the child.
- The IEP focuses more on the educational needs of the child instead of focusing on the family and the child as Early Intervention does.

• The preschool evaluation must include a test by a psychologist, which looks at the thinking and reasoning ability of the child. It also includes a complete social history.

There are other differences, but these are the most important to remember. We will spend more time discussing the details of the IEP in the next chapter, so let's get to it!

Individual Education Plan   3

Your child's Individual Education Plan (IEP) is developed in the same spirit as the Individual Family Services Plan that serves children age three and under; it is a document created by a variety of professionals and people who care about your child to prescribe specialized learning strategies and aids.

What Are Special-Education Services?

Special education is a service provided to educate children whose needs cannot be met in a regular classroom. It's as simple as that. Your child's special education can include anything from speech therapists to a special-education teacher to adjustments in the regular curriculum. It depends on the nature of your child's disability and the needs he presents.

How Does My Child Get Identified for Special Education?

Your child can be referred for special-education evaluation in a number of ways with distinctions based on the types of disability (see Table 3.1).

Table 3.1. Types of Disabilities Qualifying for Special Education

Type of Disability	Referral for Evaluation
Physical disability	Your doctor probably referred your child at a younger age for Early Intervention services, and you will transition to special-education services automatically. If your child became physically disabled after age three or was identified after age three, he will receive referrals by your doctor, school officials, yourself, family, or friends.
Learning disability	Your child's teacher was probably the first one to spot a learning disability, based on early testing or observation, and to refer your child for further evaluation. If you suspect that your child has a learning disability, you should talk to your child's teacher.
Emotional/behavioral disability	You may have already talked to your doctor or a psychologist about your child's emotional or behavioral disabilities, and they identified the problem. Many times that means your child will take medication to regulate her emotions or behavior. If your child goes to school with prescribed medication and the school has not previously identified the disability, your child will be referred for an evaluation and recommendation for special services under IDEA.

Basically, the first person who observes what they think is a potential disability needs to call their suspicion to professional attention so that your child can be referred for evaluation as soon as possible.

Your Child Has Been Identified for Special Education

What Is Your Role?

You have many roles in your child's special-education services and in the planning of them.

Team Member. You are a member of the special-education team, and it is important that you are an active member. Your child deserves your full attention with regard to the process and your assistance in implementing the plan.

Advocate. You are your child's advocate in the IEP meetings. You know and care about your child more than anyone, and you need to be active in the special-education process to protect your rights and the rights of your child.

File Clerk. There will be a lot of documentation of your child's abilities, needs, and services, and you are going to be the only member of your child's special-education team who remains on the team from year to year. You may have members of the team who are there for a few years, but no one will be there every year like you. It is up to you to maintain a complete file of your child's special-education services.

What Is the Role of the School District?

The school district bears much of the responsibility for your child's education. The law requires that your local school district provide your child with a free and appropriate public education, and it is the school district's responsibility to effectively do so.

Preparing to Write the Individual Education Plan

The Individual Education Plan (IEP) is the living document that will record the services your child will receive at school to meet his or her special-education needs. It will list achievable outcomes and the services, adaptations, or modifications that will best enable your child to achieve his learning goals.

Forming a Team

The special-education department at your local school district will select the members of your child's IEP committee, of which you will be a member. You are a valuable member of the IEP team and have the opportunity to fully participate, and the school district is responsible for making sure you understand every part of the process. Qualifications of a group member include having the appropriate professional license or certification, and may include outside practitioners when necessary. If the student requires a medical evaluation in order to determine appropriate services, the district will coordinate with you to provide that. Chances are that you have already taken your child to a medical doctor for an evaluation, and in that case you can offer to provide your physician's records. If the evaluation team determines that there is a medical question about your child's condition, the team may request that another physician examine your child.

IEP team members include

- You (the parent)
- At least one general education teacher (or preschool provider) of the student if the student is or will be participating in the general education environment
- At least one special-education teacher, or if appropriate, at least one special-education provider of the student
- A representative of the district, who is qualified to provide or supervise the provision of special education and related services, is knowledgeable about general education curriculum, and is knowledgeable about the availability of district resources
- The school psychometrist, an individual who can interpret the instructional implications of the evaluation results
- Any other individuals who have knowledge of or special expertise about the student; these individuals may be invited by either the district or the parents at the discretion of the person or party making the invitation, such as an after-school care provider, a tutor, or a medical professional
- The student, when appropriate, or when required
- Transition participants (from the Early Intervention team), when required

Preparing for the Meeting

Evaluation

The evaluation group shall use a variety of methods, tools, and strategies designed to gather relevant functional and developmental information. The evaluation does not rely on one source or procedure as the sole criterion for determination and should, to the extent available, include

- Review of existing data
- Relevant functional and developmental information
- Information from parents
- Information from other providers
- Information related to enabling access to and progress within the general education curriculum
- Current classroom-based evaluations, using criterion-referenced and curriculum-based methods, anecdotal records, and observations
- Teacher and related service providers' observations, and
- Testing and other evaluation materials, which may include medical or other evaluations when necessary.

Reevaluation

The IEP must be updated annually, although it may be revised more frequently as needed to adjust the program and services.

Every special-education student will be reevaluated at least once every three years using the evaluation procedures. Reevaluations may occur more frequently if your child's situation warrants a reevaluation or if one is requested by the parent or teacher in agreement with the district. If your child has been eligible under the category "Developmentally Delayed," he must be reevaluated before age nine to determine eligibility within another category.

As part of any reevaluation, the IEP team members, and other professionals who the district determines are appropriate, will review existing data that includes the following:

- Evaluations and information provided by you
- Current classroom-based assessments and observations
- Observations by other teachers and related service providers' data

Based on this review, the team will request any additional data required to determine:

- Whether your child continues to be eligible for special-education and any necessary related services
- The present levels of performance and educational needs, and
- Whether any additions or modifications to your child's program are needed.

After the reevaluation you should receive written notice of the following:

- Whether your child continues to be eligible and in need of special education
- Your child's present levels of performance and educational needs, and
- Whether any additions or modifications to the special-education and related services are needed to enable the student to meet IEP annual goals and to participate, as appropriate, in the general curriculum.

The IEP

Your child's IEP is based on the placement recommended by the evaluation (or reevaluation) team. There are seven placement categories designated by the Department of Education. They are the following:

1. *Special education outside the regular class less than 21 percent of the day.* Children with disabilities receiving special-education and related services outside the regular class for less than 21 percent of the school day. These children spend most of their day in the regular classroom.

2. *Special education outside the regular class at least 21 percent of the day and no more than 60 percent of the day.* Children with disabilities receiving special education and related services outside the regular class for at least 21 percent but no more than 60 percent of the school day. These children spend between 25 and 60 percent of their day in the special-education classroom.

3. *Special education outside the regular class more than 60 percent of the day.* Children with disabilities receiving special education and related services outside the regular class for more than 60 percent of the school day. These children usually spend just one or two classes outside of the special-education classroom.

4. *Public separate facility.* Children with disabilities receiving special education and related services for more than 50 percent of the school day in public separate facilities. These children spend part of the day at school and another part of their day in a special facility. These kids usually have a special need that warrants specialized treatment such as physical or occupational therapy.

5. *Private separate facility.* Children with disabilities receiving special education and related services for more than 50 percent of the school day in private separate facilities. These children spend part of the day at school and another part of their day in a special facility. These kids usually have a special need that warrants specialized treatment in a private facility.

6. *Public residential facility.* Children with disabilities receiving special education and related services for more than 50 percent of the school day in public residential facilities. These kids go to school all day at the private facility or live at the facility all or part of the time.

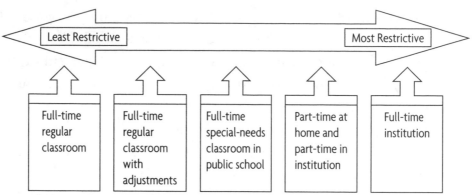

Figure 3.1. Least Restrictive to Most Restrictive Learning Environments

7. *Private residential facility.* Children with disabilities receiving special education and related services for more than 50 percent of the school day in private residential facilities.[1]

This is a good time to revisit the spectrum Least Restrictive to Most Restrictive Learning Environments (see Figure 3.1) to apply what we have just learned. Each of the categories listed above is represented here, from left to right.

In order to provide the free and appropriate education required by the law, your school district can offer a variety of special services for your child:

Special Services

- *Audiology:* determining the range, nature, and degree of hearing loss and operating programs for treatment and prevention of hearing loss

- *Counseling services:* counseling by social workers, psychologists, guidance counselors, and rehabilitation specialists

- *Early identification:* identifying a disability as early as possible in a child's life

- *Family training, counseling, and home visits:* assisting families to enhance their child's development (ages three to twenty-one only)

- *Health services:* enabling a child to benefit from other Early Intervention services (ages three to twenty-one only). These services are a continuation of a service that began as an Early Intervention service but needs to continue past age three so they become a part of the IEP.

- *Medical services:* determining a child's medically related disability that results in the child's need for special education and related services

- *Nursing services:* assessing health status; preventing health problems; and administering medications, treatments, and regimens prescribed by a licensed physician (ages three to twenty-one only)

- *Nutrition services:* conducting individual assessments to address the nutritional needs of children (ages three to twenty-one only)

- *Occupational therapy:* improving, developing, or restoring functions impaired or lost through illness, injury, or deprivation

- *Orientation and mobility services:* assisting a student to get around within various environments

- *Parent counseling and training:* providing parents with information about their child's development

- *Physical therapy:* screening, referral, and service provision for therapy regarding bone and muscle capacity and development

- *Psychological services:* administering and interpreting psychological and educational tests and other assessment procedures and managing a program of psychological services, including psychological counseling for children and parents

- *Recreation and therapeutic recreation:* assessing the child's leisure function, developing recreational programs in schools and community agencies, and providing education on leisure

- *Rehabilitative counseling services:* planning for career development, employment preparation, achieving independence, and integration in the workplace and community

- *School health services:* attending to educationally related health needs through services provided by a school nurse

- *Service coordination services:* assistance and services by a service coordinator to a child and family (ages three to twenty-one only)

- *Social work services in schools:* preparing a social or developmental history on a child, counseling groups and individuals, and mobilizing school and community resources

- *Speech pathology and speech-language pathology:* diagnosing specific speech or language impairments and giving guidance regarding them

- *Transportation and related costs:* providing travel to and from services and schools, travel in and around school buildings, and specialized equipment (for example, special or adapted buses, lifts, and ramps)

- *Assistive technology and services:* acquiring and using devices and services to restore lost capacities or improve impaired capacities

These services are components of your child's IEP. Your child's IEP team will determine, with your help, which services will best benefit your child's education.

Your IEP should include the following:

1. Your child's basic information, including assessment results, your family's concerns, and your child's strengths

2. Annual outcomes for your child to achieve through the IEP

3. The strategies and methods to be implemented to achieve the plan

4. Services your child will receive: how often, by whom, when, and where

5. The names of all of the team members, their roles, and their contact information, and

6. Next steps, including when the team will meet again.

The IEP will be written on a standard form used by your state that should include all of the information you need. You can find a sample form in Appendix B.

Implementation

Your local school district is responsible for maintaining a copy of your child's current IEP at the location or building that serves your child. The plan should be accessible to all staff members who work with your child. The building principal is usually responsible for making sure that all staff members are informed of their responsibilities and are qualified to do their job.

You will be responsible for supporting the IEP from home and working with your child to achieve learning goals. You should closely monitor your child's progress from home with activities that you implement yourself.

What's Next

We are going to cover the basics of procedural due process in Chapter Four. *Procedural due process* is a complicated legal concept that means:

1. You have the right for a procedure to occur before any of your individual rights are taken away.

2. You have the right to be notified of the procedures in plenty of time to take part in them.

3. You have the right to have someone help you understand and complete the procedures.

4. You have the right to appeal the procedures.

There are many procedures associated with protecting the rights of your special-needs child, so Chapter Four is going to be important in order to implement what you have learned about evaluations, placements, and services.

Note

1. U.S. Department of Education, Office of Special Education. (1988). *OSEP IDEA, Part B data dictionary*, 1988. Washington, DC: Author.

Procedural Due Process 4

*D*ue process is a term you have probably heard before—perhaps on a T.V. legal drama? There are two types of due process: procedural and substantive. *Substantive due process* protects the general rights that give you the power to do something, such as freedom of speech or religion. *Procedural due process* makes sure that the methods the government uses to take away a right are fair.

At this point in your life, you have no doubt become hesitant about relying on government agencies to provide special-education services, so you can understand the need for some recourse if you feel that you haven't been treated fairly. This chapter will help you ensure that your rights have been protected.

What If You and the School Disagree?

Schools have limited resources, and there is a large demand for special-education services. You may feel all alone in your quest for special services, but you aren't. Many other parents are going through the same experiences, and procedures have been set up for handling these issues. Schools are your partners in achieving an appropriate education for your child. When you are frustrated with the process, it helps to remember that it's an extremely challenging job to oversee special-education programs. Schools are dealing with the lives of children, which in turn affect the lives of their families. When schools and parents disagree about an appropriate service or educational modification, parents can quickly become emotional. This is definitely understandable, but rarely productive. It is easier for the school to disregard what you are saying if you are too emotional, believing that the source of the conflict is your lack of understanding rather than a valid concern.

What to Do If You Have a Conflict with Your Child's School District

1. *Stay calm but remain passionate.* When you disagree with the school, you are doing so in an effort to take care of your child in the best way you know how, which by definition is a passionate endeavor. School personnel are also trying to take care of your child, but they will not have the passion of a parent when doing so. The best way to communicate any important feeling about your child's education is in a calm manner. People oftentimes do not listen to others who are passionate about an issue but fail to express that passion reasonably. If you want to be heard, stay calm but remain passionate and communicate clearly.

2. *Educate.* Try to educate your school personnel about how the disability affects your child. Remember, your child's disability does not require special services unless it affects how your child learns. School officials may not be able to accurately determine whether your child is unable to benefit from her public education because they haven't been around your child as consistently as you have been. It is your job to calmly and clearly explain to the school how you feel your child should be progressing and why. Try writing a professional memo. You can find an example of one at *www.knowledgeessentials.com.*

3. *Negotiate.* Request a meeting with your school officials to discuss the matter. You should be prepared to discuss what educational goals you think your child should be able to attain and why you feel that way.

School officials will focus on whether they think your educational expectations are reasonable, what resources it will take to achieve them, and whether the school district is equipped with those resources. This is where the negotiation comes in.

Understandably, the school has practical considerations that extend beyond whether "it can be done." If you can find some middle ground between what you feel your child needs and what the school can actually provide, everyone will be a lot happier.

But what if you and the school just can't reach an agreement? There are several ways of pursuing your child's rights under IDEA.

While the information below provides a general explanation of these processes, the procedures differ in each state, and a full explanation of the rights of children and parents in this process is beyond the scope of this summary. School districts are required to provide specific information to parents about the various types of appeals and relief that may be obtained in their particular state. For additional information, see the list of state resources in Appendix C.

Due-Process Procedures Through Your School District

IDEA requires school districts to have what are known as *due-process procedures*. This is the formal process that parents and school districts can use when informal attempts to resolve a conflict have failed. For example, these procedures require that the parents be given notice of their rights at various points including when the child is evaluated or reevaluated, in notices for IEP meetings, and when the parents make a complaint.

Due-Process Appeals Through the State Education Agency

When there is disagreement over whether your child qualifies under IDEA, the content of the IEP, or your child's placement, either you or the school district may request a due-process hearing from your state's education agency.

Once such a request is filed, the school district must tell you that they can attempt to resolve the dispute through mediation if you would like to do so. Mediation is a way of trying to reach agreement with the help of a neutral party. You can refuse or mediation may not work; if that is the case, you and the school district will attend a due-process hearing to resolve the matter.

A *due-process hearing* is an administrative hearing conducted by an impartial hearing officer. Your state law sets forth exactly how this hearing process works. Remember: your school district is required to give you written information about exactly how the process works in your state.

Lawsuits

Under IDEA, you may not file a lawsuit in a court without going through the due-process appeal first. If you aren't satisfied by the results of the due-process hearing, you may sue the school district in court. The final decision from the due-process hearing, along with the record of the hearing, is then reviewed by a court.

You may consider retaining an attorney to assist you in pursuing your child's rights in a court of law. Some families find it difficult to afford an attorney, and other times it is hard to find a local attorney that understands the situation and regulations involved. Until recently, if a parent decided to take legal action against a school district, the school district would have the case dismissed if the parents didn't have an attorney. The reasoning was that parents cannot represent the rights of their child because they aren't lawyers. You can represent yourself in court, but you can't represent others unless you are a lawyer. In May 2007, the Supreme Court ruled that parents of a child with special needs don't have to hire an attorney to challenge the school district in a court of law. The Court recognized that when a school district affects the rights of a special-needs child, the school district also affects the parent's rights, so the parents are representing their own, albeit intertwined, rights when appearing in court.

Caution! The Supreme Court's ruling doesn't mean you should go out and file lawsuits just because you can represent yourself. No matter how valid your claim is, this is *very complex* legislation for anyone to interpret. As with any complex matter, engaging someone that can apply his or her experience to your unique situation is highly likely to help. The exception that the Court carved out should only be used when parents could not otherwise exercise their rights.

Types of Relief Available

If you pursue a due-process hearing, mediation, or a lawsuit, you can seek remedies such as a fully developed IEP, special-education services to make up for missed educational opportunities, and monetary reimbursement for out-of-pocket education costs. Courts may also require the school district to pay for your lawyer. There is no big cash jackpot associated with these types of lawsuits. The court's goal is equity—to try to make things right—which is why you are there anyway.

Administrative Complaint Process

What do you do if you find the education plan and IEP are satisfactory, but you believe that the school district is not complying with the agreed upon IEP? What if you believe that the school has failed to provide the procedural safeguards required for developing an IEP? Both of these situations can be challenged through the *administrative complaint process*. This process is different from the due-process hearing described above. Each state is required to establish written procedures for resolving these kinds of complaints. The procedures include an independent investigation and a written decision within a certain amount of time.

Complaints are usually filed with your state's special-education office. If the information for filing a complaint is not supplied to you by your school district, call one of the state resources listed in Appendix C.

If you file an administrative complaint, the school district may be ordered by the state or federal education agency to take corrective action, including following specific instructions for developing a proper IEP or reimbursing you for out-of-pocket education costs, such as tutoring or summer school. In certain circumstances, an administrative complaint may be appealed in court.

Is It Possible to Win a Due-Process Hearing?

Of course it's possible to win a due-process hearing, especially if you are in the right. It's also possible to lose a due-process hearing, even if you are right. There are some things you can do to help yourself.

1. *Professionalism.* You will best represent yourself and your child if you do so in as professional a manner as possible. You are going to be negotiating, and that is best done with documentation, not emotion. For example, your child's school district may not think your child's diabetes qualifies for special services. Remember, a disability only qualifies for special services if it affects your child's ability to benefit from her education. To properly negotiate a solution with your child's school district, you should be prepared to demonstrate:

- How the diabetes impacts your child's educational goals
- Which service(s) you are requesting
- Examples of similar circumstances that have worked with other children or other schools

Negotiating is a give-and-take process, and there is a fine line between asking for more than you want, in order to have "room to go down," and asking for so much that you will not be taken seriously. There can be no negotiation unless both parties come to the table. In this situation, unlike most business situations, both sides are in it for the same goal: to help your child. I suggest proposing what you really think your child needs and negotiating a way you can get there together.

2. *Paper trail.* The most important thing you can do is to carefully document every part of this process. A paper trail may not seem necessary during the school years that run smoothly, but stay consistent and keep collecting the information. The documents from years that go well are actually documenting the services that positively impact your child's education. If you enter into a school year that is bumpy for your child, these documents can show school personnel how to make adjustments to your child's special services.

You need to keep such documents as:

- Test scores (including how your child was assessed)
- Test information (what kind of test it was and what it measured)
- Medical history
- Examples of classroom work
- All IEP notices
- All IEP forms
- The final IEP

3. *Appearance.* I'm not suggesting a fancy suit here, but it is important to present yourself in a neat, clean, and professional manner. There are two important reasons for this. First, no matter which side of the debate you fall on with respect to this issue, the fact is that your appearance affects how people listen to you and treat you. Second, if you walk into the meeting or school office in sweats or in your pajamas (yes, I have personally witnessed parents arriving at morning meetings in pajamas), you will not be taken seriously and people will not listen to you. Think about it: If you didn't care enough to take the time to dress for a meeting, you probably didn't take the time to properly understand the issues you are meeting about.

4. *Expectations.* As parents you want "the best" for your child, but you also need to manage your expectations with what the school

district will provide. If you walk in and say that the school has to provide "the best" possible education for your child, you've just lost your case. The law does not entitle special-education students to what's "best," but rather to what will meet that student's "unique needs" and provide "educational benefits." IDEA guarantees nothing more than a Free Appropriate Public Education (FAPE).

Setting reasonable expectations for the process and the services and understanding that your efforts contribute to your child's education will prepare you for the road ahead and give you the strength of resolve to maintain your effort.

5. *Get a lawyer.* Special-education law is confusing, and you aren't expected to know the nuances of the legislative pieces that affect your daily life. If you encounter a situation that involves substantive legal issues, get a lawyer.

The Special-Needs Classroom   11

The Regular Classroom Versus the Special-Needs Classroom

5

How do you know when your child should be in a regular classroom or a special-needs classroom? How can you make that decision, or agree with the IEP team decision if you don't know more about it? What are the similarities and differences between the environments?

When Your Child Should Be in a Special-Needs Classroom

A key concept in special education is that children with disabilities should, to the maximum extent possible, be educated with their non-disabled peers, or as the law puts it, in the least restrictive environment. The only time a child should be placed in a setting away from the general education population is when he or she cannot be educated in a regular classroom even with accommodations or modifications such as supplementary aids and services. There are times when skill deficits require direct, individualized instruction that is best delivered in a small setting, oftentimes one-on-one.

Special-education services can be divided into two types of settings: traditional and inclusive. A traditional setting is one in which children with disabilities attend special-education classes with other disabled children. Can that happen with the requirement for the least restrictive environment? The legal requirement does not mean that one size fits all.

A percentage of preschool or kindergarten children with disabilities may not function well in the inclusive classroom. Their emotional or physical characteristics may require individualized and small-group experiences in a self-contained class. These classes are comprised solely of special-needs kids. These children receive direct instruction from teachers trained in their special needs. In a self-contained classroom, fewer opportunities exist for children to interact with typically developing peers, who can model skills and behavior. These programs are usually best for children with physical or emotional disabilities. For example, traditional settings for children who are deaf, blind, or have orthopedic disabilities develop your child's life skills and could be necessary to maintain the level of medical care required for your child's health and safety.

Preschool and Elementary School

In a special-education classroom, you will see no more than ten students receiving instruction at a time. This allows the special-education teacher to provide intense instruction in areas of behavior and learning. You will see children learning different concepts at different instructional levels. This is achieved through individual or small-group lessons. Your child will receive instruction that will help him to meet goals and objectives described in his IEP. Most special-education teachers have at least one paraprofessional (specially trained teacher's aide) to assist them in their classroom.

Middle School and High School

The middle school special-needs classroom shifts from the typical "pullout" model of the elementary schools to a variety of options at the middle school. Remember the Least Restrictive Environment spectrum?

It is best to provide education in which a student with a disability can participate in the general curriculum with his peers to the maximum extent possible. There are times when the general education classroom cannot meet the needs of a student with a disability, even with accommodations or modifications. The nature and severity of disabilities is considered, and you and the IEP team will determine what is appropriate for your teen.

When to Include Your Child in the Regular Classroom

Your child should be in the regular classroom as much as her disability will allow her to be in one. Inclusion is a philosophy founded on the belief that all children, disabled or not, can learn; and they benefit from learning, working, and playing together. For disabled students it means being educated in classes with children without disabilities, as appropriate. It also means providing important supports and services that enable them to benefit from these classes. Supports and services that are sometimes needed may include modifying or adapting the curriculum, activities, materials, or adjusting schedules. It can also include certain types of appropriate staffing (special-education teacher coteaching), special instructional strategies, and related services. Related services are developmental, corrective, and other support services that are required to assist a child with a disability to benefit from instruction. Examples of related services are speech/language therapy; physical and or occupational therapy; vision services; specialized equipment, technology or other materials; assistance from a nurse or aide; and transportation services.

The inclusion of children with disabilities in all grade levels is becoming more and more common. Parents, teachers, and researchers have found that children benefit in many ways from integrated programs that are designed to meet the needs of all children. Many children with disabilities, however, need accommodations to participate successfully in the general classroom. To help you make the best possible general educational placement decision, here are a few things to consider.

1. How well informed is the general education teacher regarding your child's disability? Does the teacher demonstrate knowledge about your child's disability? Is the teacher open to collaborative ideas?

2. What is the teacher's basic philosophy regarding students with disabilities and her attitude regarding the strategies and techniques that are effective for your child?

3. Does she take a passive or tolerant approach to disabled students in the general classroom or does she take an active responsible role? Is the general education teacher innovative with instructional approaches?

Choosing an informed general education teacher sets the stage for a productive partnership and a more positive, less frustrating school experience for your child. It is important for your child to be in the regular classroom for as much of the school day as possible. Communicate with your child's teachers and the IEP team about this to help determine the proper amount of time for your child to be in the regular classroom. As a high school student it is more critical than ever for your child to be a part of normal social environments and experience the normal expectations as much as possible.

Let's look at the different ways your child can be part of the regular classroom.

Preschool

For preschoolers, inclusion occurs through:

A special-education preschool that includes children without disabilities. Disabled children and low-income preschoolers from the Head Start program are often combined in one class. Your child receives individualized attention, plus the chance to interact with nondisabled peers. "Research shows that inclusive settings benefit special-needs kids by providing positive role models and improving socialization and behavior," says Samuel L. Odom, Ph.D., Otting Professor of Special Education at Indiana University in Bloomington.

A traditional community preschool, with support services. Your child attends a mainstream community preschool, and your school district provides a special-education teacher to act as a consultant there. That teacher meets with the preschool staff regularly to modify the program to meet your child's needs. Sometimes the district also provides free speech, occupational, or physical therapy at the preschool. "When appropriate support is in place, this is one of the best choices for kids who don't have severe disabilities," says Dr. Beverly. However, you will be responsible for at least some of the cost. School districts don't usually pay for private programs, although they may cover a portion of the tuition.

Public preschool. Most states now offer public preschool programs. The number of classes in the program will depend on your local school district, as some districts implement new programs such as this in stages. Since your child will have an IEP, make sure a public classroom education is written into the plan and that your child will have access to even small preschool programs.

Combination plans. If your school district offers you a half-day special-education class, consider supplementing it with another half-day program in a traditional community preschool. Your child will benefit from tuition-free, individualized instruction in the special-education program, and socialization with nondisabled kids in the community program.

Elementary School

Special-education classrooms should be located among the general education classrooms. These settings are designed to be conducive to small-group learning. The special-education teacher is trained in innovative instructional strategies, behavior management techniques, and learning styles. They are generalists in the subject areas, but are trained to apply methods and strategies that will assist your child in developing skills. Special-education teachers have extensive knowledge in many areas of disabilities and understand the laws and procedures that govern special education. The No Child Left Behind Act does require that all teachers, including special-education teachers, be or become "highly qualified" in the subject areas they teach, but this is more of a concern for the upper grade levels where subject areas become more specific and the depth of content knowledge is deeper.

Your child may receive service in this setting for most of his day or may only attend the special-education classroom, often called the resource room, for instruction in only one subject area.

Some ways inclusion occurs for elementary school children are as follows:

1. *General education class with accommodations and consultation services.* Students participate in all general education classes with accommodations. A special-education IEP administrator monitors grades and progress closely.

2. *General education classes with accommodations with a special-education coteacher or team teacher.* A special-education teacher teaches with the general education teacher and specializes in learning styles and instructional approaches, and is knowledgeable in accommodations for special-needs students. All students receive instruction and assistance from both teachers.

3. *Resource room or lab room for specialized instruction for a percentage of the day.* Some students need specialized instruction in math only or perhaps just language arts. Specialized and individualized instruction can be designed in these classes. A student who needs specialized instruction in math may attend the lab or resource room for one period a day and be in general education classes for the

remainder of his instruction. Students pass from one class to the other and are not "pulled out" of another classroom.

An elementary school resource room is likely to seem a little like a preschool classroom because the children are often still trying to attain some of the developmental milestones that children without special needs have already achieved. Many people don't realize that resource rooms can also look more colorful than other rooms in the school, and they may be equipped with objects that look like toys but are really being used as learning aids. Colorful and engaging rooms are also important learning tools that are used to stimulate children and engage them in the environment.

You are likely to see at least one teacher aide in the resource room at all times.

4. *A self-contained classroom is the most restrictive placement and is used when a student's disability severely impacts his educational performance.* Self-contained classrooms provide structure and regularity for students who may have difficulty with adaptive skills. The curriculum is usually focused on gaining and learning functional skills. If the school has more than three or four students who are diagnosed with severe emotional disturbances or severe behavior problems due to neurological or physical disabilities, it will probably have a dedicated self-contained room just for those students with at least one teacher aide.

Middle School and High School

A regular classroom in middle school is much more like a high school classroom than an elementary classroom. Your child will be changing classes and will for the first time be able to choose some of the classes that comprise his schedule. If your child is attending a regular class most or all of the day, it is because of the accommodations or modifications that are made in the regular classroom.

We will describe a few typical secondary approaches to meeting a student's needs. Schools may call these options different names, but this will give you an idea of the options relating to the Least Restrictive Enviroment (LRE) spectrum that was discussed in Chapter Three, beginning with the least restrictive and moving to the most restrictive.

Some ways inclusion occurs for middle and high school students are the following:

1. *General education class with accommodations and consultation services.* Students participate in all general education classes with accommodations. A special-education IEP administrator monitors grades and progress closely.

2. *General education classes with accommodations with a special-education coteacher or team teacher.* A special-education teacher teaches with the general education teacher and specializes in learning styles and instructional approaches, and is knowledgeable in accommodations for special-needs students. All students receive instruction and assistance from both teachers.

3. *Resource room or lab room for specialized instruction for a percentage of the day.* Some students need specialized instruction in math only or perhaps just language arts. Specialized and individualized instruction can be designed in these classes. A student who needs specialized instruction in math may attend the lab or resource room for one period a day and be in general education classes for the remainder of his instruction. Students pass from one class to the other and are not "pulled out" of another classroom.

Resource rooms for middle school students may have some seemingly childish features, but for the most part begin to take on more characteristics of the regular classroom. There is a lower ratio of technology and other resources available for students than there is in the regular classroom, which may even approach 1:1 in some cases.

4. *A self-contained classroom is the most restrictive placement and is used when a student's disability severely impacts his educational performance.* Self-contained classrooms provide structure and regularity

for students who may have difficulty with adaptive skills. The curriculum is usually focused on gaining and learning functional skills. Like elementary schools, if the middle or high school has more than three or four students who are diagnosed with severe emotional disturbances or severe behavior problems due to neurological or physical disabilities, it will probably have a dedicated self-contained room just for those students with at least one teacher aide. As the students get older and grow larger, the physical presence of teacher aides is very useful.

How Do I Decide Which Setting Is More Appropriate for My Child?

There is no magic formula for determining which educational environment is the most appropriate for your child. If there was, then there would never be a problem with a child's placement. Since it is impossible to know whether you have made the right decision prior to placing your child in an educational environment, the least restrictive environment continuum is your best friend. Always err of the side of the least restrictive environment that you and the IEP team are considering. If you question whether your child should be in an inclusive environment for half of the school day or for all of the school day, start with placing your child in the inclusive classroom for the entire day and move toward the special-needs classroom placement if your child demonstrates the need (either with behavior, classroom performance, or both).

Tips for Buying Educational Products or Toys for Your Special-Needs Child

A common tendency for anyone with children, disabled or not, is to buy everything in sight that may help their child learn. There are a few things you need to keep in mind when buying educational products or toys for your disabled child:

1. *Potential for interaction.*

    Will your child be an active participant when playing with the toy? Will the toy encourage social interaction with others?

    You want the toy to require or promote activity with other children. Your child needs to interact with children her own age. Inabilities to socialize are components of many disabilities: physical, learning, and especially emotional/behavioral. While it is important to have toys that engage your child in solitary play, they should be utilized only when there are no other children to play with or to redirect frustration when playing with a group becomes too much for your child.

2. *Opportunities for success.*

    Can the toy promote open-ended play with no definite right or wrong way? For example, building blocks or crayons are open-ended toys, while board games have a definite right and wrong way to play. If there is a definite right or wrong, is it within your child's skill level at least part of the time? Is it adaptable to suit your child's special needs?

    It is important that your child experience success in play, but also that she experience the pressure-free environment created by open-ended play.

3. *Developmental age.*

    Is the toy compatible with your child's developmental age without being too far off his chronological age?

    The more severe the discrepancy between your child's developmental age and chronological age, the more difficult it will be to buy toys that don't seem too young. This is a fine line that can only be drawn with the personality traits of your child.

4. *Self-Expression.*

Are there opportunities for creativity, uniqueness, and choice when playing with the toy?

Like all children, those with special needs should be given the opportunity for creativity and unique interpretation when playing. These skills are essential for your child's emotional and educational growth.

5. *Media.*

Will your child experience a variety of media when playing with the toy?

Does playing with the toy involve action figures and a book? Play dough and crayons? Television and a board game?

Exposing children to a variety of types of toys is important to foster self-expression and imagination.

6. *Current popularity.*

Is this a toy that would be popular with any child? Does it tie in with current TV shows, movies, books, or video games?

Your child will feel more socially connected to his peers if he can experience the same pop culture that all kids his age are enjoying.

Accommodations and Modifications

6

The general education classroom's inclusive environment has great potential to meet your child's educational needs when you as a parent know what teacher and classroom characteristics are conducive to your child's needs. A primary goal of IDEA is to make certain that students with disabilities are educated to the full extent of their abilities and participate with typical peers, which is accomplished through accommodations and modifications. *Accommodations* and *modifications* are often terms that are mistakenly used synonymously, particularly when your child gets older. It is important to know the difference because your teen's access to the general curriculum can be affected.

An *accommodation* is defined as a support or service that is provided to help a student fully access the general education curriculum or subject matter. Students with impaired spelling or handwriting skills, for example, may be accommodated by a note taker or receive permission to take class notes on a laptop computer. An accommodation does not change the content of what is being taught or the expectation that the student meet a performance standard applied for all students.

There are also several classroom characteristics to consider that can be adjusted through accommodations. For example, your child's seating arrangement can be an important factor. Consider requesting preferential seating such as the seat closest to where the teacher does most of the instructing. This helps keep your child on task and makes it easier for the teacher to monitor your child. A well-organized and predictable classroom is important because it provides consistency and structure for a child with a disability. Children with disabilities are more likely to take educational risks when an emotionally safe and equitable classroom is established.

A *modification* is defined as a change to the general education curriculum or other material being taught, which alters the standards or expectations for students with disabilities. Your child may not be required to meet the same curriculum content and skill requirements as children without special needs. Instruction can be modified so that the material is presented differently or the expectations of what the student will master are changed. A modification can also be made in which the physical environment is changed to meet your child's needs, and the curriculum content and skill goals stay the same as those for children without special needs. Modifications are not allowed in most postsecondary education environments.

Assistive technology is defined as any device that helps a student with a disability function in a given environment, but does not limit the device to expensive or "high-tech" options. Assistive technology can also include simple devices such as laminated pictures for communication, removable highlighter tapes, Velcro, and other "low-tech" devices.

Let's take a look at the factors that can help your child stay in the inclusive environment as much of the day as possible. Here are some lists of accommodations and modifications that can enable your child to complete grade-level curriculum expectations.

Preschool

Accommodations

- Creative play activities, nursery rhymes, classic children's literature and fairy tales, folk songs, and bedtime songs on cassette.
- Visual prompts such as flash cards or number lines
- Pictorial calendars and schedules
- Alphabet and nursery-rhyme books
- Scratch-and-sniff books and puzzles
- Touch-and-feel books with moving parts and touch activities
- Dramatized book and CD/cassette combinations
- Timers as a cue to begin or end an activity
- Multisensory approaches (see, say, write in the air, trace with a pencil)
- A structured environment
- Predictable rules and routines
- Consistent rewards for appropriate behavior
- Behavior management techniques such as positive reinforcement and time-outs

Modifications

- More frequent bathroom breaks
- Napping
- Systematic teaching of social skills
- Supportive therapies using music and art
- Relaxation techniques
- Self-management strategies

Elementary School

Accommodations

Presentation

- Use multisensory teaching (see, say, write in the air, trace with a pencil)
- Use manipulatives to make learning more concrete
- Change the order of an assignment or test
- Use xerox copies, rather than dittos; many children have difficulty reading blue/purple print
- Avoid using fluorescent or glossy paper
- Provide adequate space to separate the lines of text
- Use different color papers for different worksheets or handouts
- Teach new vocabulary words at the beginning of the activity
- Read directions or worksheets to the child; have the child paraphrase the passage to check comprehension

Responding

- Use a computer
- Dictate answers
- Draw a response
- Color-code answers with colored pencils or pens

Timing

- Extend the time to complete an assignment or test
- Allow for frequent breaks

Setting

- Work on assignments with a small group
- Take tests in a quiet room that is removed from other students and distractions
- Seat child in an area free from distractions with access to peer tutors and special equipment (from a computer to colored textbook overlays)
- Use preferential seating (for example, in the front, close to the teacher, or close to the peer tutor)
- Seat child near natural light; reduce exposure to fluorescent lighting
- Use colored textbook overlays of the child's choice, if helpful, to cut down on glare (often useful are smoky, blue-gray, pink, yellow, and red)

Modifications

Presentation

- Provide visual cues (for example, charts, pictures, and graphs)
- Use enlarged print
- Simplify directions, making them more step-by-step in format
- Number sentences in directions
- Provide a box or line to the left of each direction or step to check off as each is completed
- Highlight or underline the verbs in directions (for example, add numbers, circle the correct answer)
- Provide pictures, illustrations, or diagrams of individual steps in the activity

Timing

- Eliminate or limit timed tasks to skills and knowledge the student has mastered

Setting

- Give the child a number line and alphabet strip on his or her desk to use as a reference to correctly form letters and numbers

- Have the child keep a list of key words (for example, bed, pet, quick, good), which contain letters she reverses, to use as a reference when writing

- Place a piece of green tape on the left edge of the child's desk to remind him to begin work at the left

- Allow the use of a "word window" (a card with a hole that has been cut out so that only a single word is viewable at a time through the window)

Assignments

- Modify spelling assignments: (1) use a regular class list to develop meaning; (2) use words from the child's structured, synthetic phonics reading program to promote spelling the same patterns that she is learning to read

- Use cooperative learning where a peer or parent reads text selections or math story problems to the child and the child answers questions

- Reduce paper and pencil tasks by 50 percent

- Use taped stories where the child follows along with the book (for voice-print match and learning of high-frequency words)

- Use taped textbooks and taped assignments, as needed

- Avoid having the child read or spell aloud in front of the class unless the child volunteers

- Cue the child, when necessary
- Reduce the length or modify the method of completing assignments, including homework (fewer questions or problems; book report on tape)
- Provide graph paper (large block) for math assignments
- Mark the place on the page where the child is to start the assignment, using tape/marker/highlighter
- Permit the child to choose cursive writing or printing
- Highlight or circle reversals and transpositions for correction, but do not count them as wrong
- Provide copies of transparencies and assignments presented on the blackboard; do not require the child to copy them
- Require the student to "proofread" aloud (or in a whisper) all written work

Testing Adaptations

- Test orally
- Use reduced reading-level tests
- Replace tests with oral reports or projects
- Provide practice tests when possible
- Use spelling words that test the knowledge of specific features (for example, CVC, CVCe) rather than subject matter or typical vocabulary
- Have the child spell orally and correct any misspelled written words before assigning a grade
- Administer a test at a specific time of day and in several timed sessions or, if lengthy, over several days
- Allow subtests to be taken in a different order so that your child can begin the test with a section in which he is likely to be successful,

rather than becoming frustrated from the beginning and having that "spill over" to affect performance on the sections where your child would be more comfortable

Grading

- Give credit for projects
- Award credit for class participation
- Reduce the weight of written tests
- Provide more multiple-choice tests
- Grade for content, not spelling

Physical Setting

- Make use of preferential seating, for example, seated near the front of the room and away from distractions if such a location helps him maintain better focus
- Modular seating is a flexible arrangement in which desks are grouped to allow students to work together. This is a great solution for some students with disabilities, as it enables peer interaction and allows the teacher to spend time with groups of students while letting the rest of the class work uninterrupted.
- Use switches and timers to help children with motor problems run electrical or battery-powered toys
- Incorporate touch puzzles with high-contrast colors and textures to teach the concepts of basic shapes and to develop motor skills; use multicolored foam letters and numbers
- Use a sensory stimulation kit with tactile-kinesthetic and auditory components; provide games, puzzles, and toys that will develop fine motor skills, visual functioning, measurement concepts, and identification skills

- Use adaptive tricycles, scooters, and walkers; balls with sounds; and toys with other adaptive features

- Employ adaptive equipment including an adjustable easel, special swings and frames, stands, mats, walkers, prone stander, chairs with trays, and pencil grips

- Provide ready access to desks, sensory tables, and computers

As your child gets older, she may require different types of accommodations or modifications in order to be successful. These adjustments are significant not only because of the success they help create in the school environment, but also because they are the basis by which your child will develop his own accommodations and modifications that he will use after he graduates from high school.

Middle School and High School

Accommodations

Presentation

- Stand near the student when giving instructions

- Put the daily routine in writing where it's easy to see

- Allow the tape recording of lectures

- Provide a written outline of the material covered in the class

- Use an overhead projector and other visual media to display notes with oral instruction

- When the teacher is using the visual media, provide a printed copy of what is being displayed

- Incorporate technology, for example, computers, calculators, and videos

Communication

- Develop a daily or weekly home-to-school communication system, such as notes, checklists, voice mail, or e-mail
- Mail assignment sheets directly to the student's home
- Hold periodic student-teacher meetings
- Provide a written explanation of homework assignments
- Give reminders about due dates for long-term assignments

Assignments

- Accept typed or word-processed assignments
- Allow oral or audio-taped submission of assignments
- Individualize assignments, for example, length, number, due date, and topic

Testing Adaptations

- Give open-book tests
- Allow one page of notes to be used during testing
- Vary the format of the test
- Read the questions aloud
- Allow the student to respond to questions orally in another room
- Provide extra time to complete the test
- Give parts of the test in more than one sitting
- Allow for the opportunity to take the test in another room or at another time of day
- Allow the student to retake the test
- Give more frequent short quizzes and fewer long tests

Grading

- Give credit for projects
- Give credit for class participation
- Reduce the weight of written tests
- Provide more multiple-choice tests
- Base grades on modified standards, for example, IEP objectives, effort, amount of improvement, content rather than spelling
- Specify the skills he has mastered rather than giving a letter grade
- Mark the correct answers rather than the mistakes
- Develop a reward system for work completed and turned in
- Grade for content on writing assignments, not spelling

Peer Involvement

- Use peer tutoring
- Select a "study buddy" who can copy assignments or clarify them by phone

Physical Setting

- Use preferential seating, for example, seated near the front of the room and away from distractions if such a location helps him maintain better focus
- Include opportunities for physical activity in the schedule

Modifications

- Allow extra credit assignments
- Allow him to work on homework at school in order to provide him with extra time

- Provide extra practice questions for study
- Limit homework to a certain amount of time spent productively, rather than an amount of work to be completed
- Give modified assignments

Administration

7

As the parent of a child with disabilities, you are responsible for a host of administrative matters that are central to managing your child's disability. There are meetings, doctor appointments, special services, and the list goes on. The best thing you can do is to start an organizational system when your child is young and maintain it throughout your child's education. Organization will serve you well and is half the battle. Wouldn't you hate it if someone misplaced a single test result and your child had to retake an evaluation? It could be painful for your child, it would be a hassle for you, and everyone's time would definitely be better spent.

You are going to get paperwork from several people and places as well as having paperwork mailed to you. Some examples are the following:

Medical paperwork. Your child may have many doctor appointments to address medical needs associated with her disability, and you will need to keep a file containing the diagnosis, insurance documents, and both historical and active prescription medicines. You also need to keep copies of your child's eyeglasses prescriptions or other adaptive devices' specifications.

Your child will see a medical doctor for diagnosis associated with special services evaluations, and you should keep a record of which diagnostic tests your child has taken along with the results of those tests.

Educational paperwork. Along with medical evaluations, your child will have many other evaluations that help determine exactly what skills your child has and has not mastered. Like medical evaluations, these tests help educators determine which combination of learning devices will most assist your child's academic achievement. It is important to maintain complete records of your child's school performance; your family may move to a neighborhood in a different school district, and it helps to have the paperwork when your child moves from one grade to the next. You never know if the same special-education coordinator will work with your child from year to year, and the minute you count on the school to maintain complete records, something will get lost.

Special-services paperwork. There will be a lot of special-services paperwork. Your school district is required by law to properly serve your child's educational needs, and as such they thoroughly document all communication, meetings, and parental requests. Along with the IEP paperwork you will receive when you attend the placement meeting, you can expect to receive notices in the mail such as:

- *Notice of Proposed School District Action.* Written notice to you if your child's placement is changed within the guidelines of the IEP or if your child is disciplined.

- *Evaluation Consent Form.* Seeks your consent to test your child for more accurate placement or to initiate the placement process.

- *Notice of School District Refusal to Act.* Basically a denial of accommodations or services.

- *Meeting invitation.* Requests your attendance at a meeting.

- *Attendance sheet.* Records who attends each meeting.

You can find more examples of paperwork you will see in meetings in Appendix B and at www.knowledgeessentials.com.

Meetings

Elementary School Meetings

You will attend many meetings if your child is referred for special services for the first time at any age. Your child will be evaluated by school officials and perhaps by experts in your community who will require you to make the appointments and take your child to the evaluations. There may be medical appointments and a host of other meetings associated with your child's new diagnosis.

Communication and collaboration are essential elements for the success of your child. Meetings are often a good way to include everyone involved in educating your child. This is a time to celebrate progress and accomplishments and to address any concerns. Meetings go beyond the annual IEP meeting or review and extend to parent-teacher conferences. The following are a few tips that can help you meet with school personnel in a way that establishes a productive relationship:

- Help the teacher get to know your child.
- Be collaborative.
- Communicate, communicate, communicate!
- Be even-tempered.
- Put it in writing.
- Join forces with the teacher to help your child become organized.
- Participate in the classroom.
- Stretch the teacher's awareness of learning and attention problems.
- Know your rights and responsibilities.

Middle and High School Meetings

Middle school IEP meetings are the building blocks to a successful outcome of your child's free and appropriate public education. As your child enters middle school, you will find the IEP team is focused on helping your child adapt to a more independent environment. By your child's last year in middle school, the IEP team will start focusing on the transition planning that will be a part of the team's focus throughout the remainder of your child's education. Middle school is also a time to really start involving your child in whether certain types of modifications and services may still be needed, as well as his long-term goals that will impact transition planning.

High school IEP meetings can be a time for celebrating accomplishments and looking at the prospects for your teen's future. IEP meetings can also be a teaching and learning tool for your teen. Meetings are a time for your teen to develop a firm understanding of her disability and her strengths and challenges. This is an important time for your teen to begin sharing her interests and preferences in course work and her future plans. IEP meetings should begin to change from adult-directed to student-directed. This transformation should begin to empower your teen and promote self-determination and self-advocacy. Help your teen to understand the components of an IEP and the educational terminology that is used. It is especially important for you both to understand transition planning in order to maximize the services, supports, and activities that will help your teen be prepared for the future. Not only should teens actively participate in the IEP process required meetings but in any meeting that can help develop self-advocacy skills.

Paperwork

Elementary School Paperwork

Get a filing cabinet and get ready. There is extensive paperwork associated with the entire process. Your best bet is to categorize your paperwork and then add to the different types each year. Categories may include: IEPs,

Eye Doctor, Transportation Services, Physical Therapy . . . you get the idea; then file the paperwork by year in each category.

In this chapter, we have not described a lot of paperwork or procedural issues but focused more on characteristics, accommodations, and helpful tips. However, it is necessary for you to understand the procedures and paperwork involved when your child is eligible for and receives special-education services.

If your child has been determined as eligible to receive special-education services, begin to educate yourself by learning as much about special education as you can. Specifically, understand the IEP process and services and supports that are available through your local school district and state agencies.

Your child's IEP will be developed annually. You are expected to be an active participant in this process. In order to actively participate, you must know the components of the IEP and what each component should address and explain (see Chapter Three). You will be expected to keep up with:

- Your child's IEP documentation

- Your child's medical records

- Any paperwork related to the special services your child is receiving from the school district

- You child's evaluation results

- Samples of your child's school work

Middle School and High School Paperwork

IEP. Your child's IEP continues to be reviewed annually or more often if needed. However, a few paperwork requirements are different at the high school level. High school typically begins when students turn sixteen and transition planning commences. Students under age sixteen usually do not have transition plans, so this is probably a new component to your teen's IEP. Be familiar with the critical elements of the transition plan. During transition planning, your teen will be informed, no later than age seventeen, of any transferable rights at the age of majority. Simply stated, on the eighteenth birthday, your teen is no longer a minor and has the right to inspect all educational records that pertain to his education. It is important to know your state's guidelines regarding the age of majority.

Transition plan. Transition services are a plan or blueprint containing long-term goals and a coordinated set of activities and services designed to promote a successful transition away from the special services provided by the school district. Transition services are required to begin by age sixteen; however, depending on your child's needs, transition services may begin earlier.

Summary of performance. A new paperwork requirement under IDEA 2004 states that all special-education students who leave secondary education through graduation or by exceeding the state age eligibility are to be provided with a Summary of Performance (SOP). The SOP is to be developed in lieu of an exit IEP. This summary should provide relevant, current, and meaningful information about your teen's educational performance that will be useful in transitioning into the postsecondary world.

The Summary of Performance, with the accompanying documentation, is important in assisting the student in the transition from high school to higher education, training, or employment. This information is necessary under Section 504 of the Rehabilitation Act and the Americans with Disabilities Act to help establish a student's eligibility for reasonable accommodations and supports in postsecondary settings. It is also useful for the Vocational Rehabilitation Comprehensive Assessment process, which is similar to the diagnostic tests taken during the evaluative process and tells us what disability your child has. The Vocational Rehabilitation Comprehensive Assessment process helps target your child's current level of functioning to help institutions consider accommodations for access. These recommendations should not imply that any individual who qualified for special education in high school would automatically qualify for services in postsecondary education or the employment setting. Postsecondary settings will continue to make eligibility decisions for services on a case-by-case basis.

The SOP is most useful when linked with the IEP process and your child has the opportunity to actively participate in the development of this document.

The SOP *must* be completed during the final year of high school. The timing of the completion of the SOP may vary depending on your child's postsecondary goals. If transitioning to higher education, the SOP, with additional documentation, may be necessary when you apply to a college or university. Likewise, this information may be necessary when applying for services from state agencies such as vocational rehabilitation. In some instances, it may be most appropriate to wait until the spring of a student's final year to provide an agency or employer the most updated information on performance.

An SOP contains the following parts:

Part One: Background information. Complete this section as specified. Please note this section also requests that you attach copies of the most recent formal and informal assessment reports documenting the student's disability or functional limitations and provide information to assist in post–high-school planning.

Part Two: Student's postsecondary goals. These goals should indicate the environment(s) that your child intends to transition to upon completion of high school.

Part Three: Summary of performance. This section includes three critical areas: academic, cognitive, and functional levels of performance. Next to each specified area, please complete the student's present level of performance and the accommodations, modifications, and assistive technology that were *essential* in high school to assist the student in achieving progress. Please leave blank any section that is not applicable.

To review what was discussed in Chapter Six, an *accommodation* is a support or service that is provided to help a student fully access the general education curriculum or subject matter, but does not change the content of what is being taught or the expectation that the student meet the general performance standard. A *modification* is a change to the curriculum or other material that alters the standards or expectations for students with disabilities. The material is presented differently or the expectations of what the student will master are changed; however, modifications are not allowed in most postsecondary education institutions. *Assistive technology* is a device that helps a student with a disability function in a given environment.

The completion of this section may require the input from a number of school personnel including the special-education teacher, regular education teacher, school psychologist, or related services personnel. It is recommended, however, that one individual from the IEP Team be responsible for gathering and organizing the information required on the SOP.

Part Four: Recommendations to assist the student in meeting postsecondary goals. This section should present suggestions for accommodations, adaptive devices, assistive services, compensatory strategies, and collateral support services for enhancing access in a post–high-school environment, including higher education, training, employment, independent living, and community participation.

Summary of Performance: Student Perspective

Student input (highly recommended). It is highly recommended that this section be completed and that the student provide information related to this Summary of Performance. The student's contribution can help (a) secondary professionals complete the summary, (b) your child to better understand the impact of her disability on academic and functional performance in the postsecondary setting, and (c) postsecondary personnel to more clearly understand your child's strengths and the impact of the disability on him. This section may be filled out independently by the student or completed with the student through an interview.

Special-Needs Tips by Grade Level   III

Preschool to Kindergarten   8

Sending your child to school for the first time can be traumatic for you and your child. It's a huge change in the routine, a watershed moment, really. How will your child get to school? Will he be home for lunch? What is the building like? How many teachers will interact with her during the day? How close is your child's classroom to the fifth-grade classroom? Where's the bathroom? What about the water fountain? Is the school on a busy street? How is recess monitored? What happens in case of an emergency?

The best way to start any new school year is to take a tour. You should have a chance to tour your child's school at the open house or during the enrollment period. If you can't make it to school at that time, or if you just can't wait any longer to see the building, call the school. Someone at the school, most likely your child's teacher, will make time to show you around and allay some of your fears.

As all coaches know though, the best defense is a good offense. So let's spend some time on the basic skills that will make being a preschooler or kindergartener much easier.

Building-Block Skills

Your child has special needs and that can mean that she communicates too often and too loudly or that she doesn't communicate much at all. Either way your child needs some basic communication skills to be successful at school. School is 100 percent about giving and receiving communication, so this is the basic skill that we are going to cover in this chapter.

Talking

Communicating wants and needs is an important part of being ready to start school. Your child should be able to say to his teacher that he needs to go to the bathroom, he needs a drink of water, he needs supplies (a new piece of paper, for example), and that another child is bothering him. You can help your child gain the confidence to clearly state his wants and needs by:

1. *Visiting.* When you take your child to a friend or relative's house, encourage your child to talk to the host if she needs to use the bathroom or wants a drink of water. Your child will probably tell you first and that will give you the opportunity to prompt your child to communicate her needs.

2. *Backing off.* When your child is playing at home let him need something. Being a good parent isn't anticipating all of your child's needs, sometimes it is about letting your child need more cereal and letting him ask you for it. Remember, this is your first opportunity to teach your child how you want him to speak to others when you are not around!

3. *Encouraging the child to speak to many adults.* There is a fine line to tread here and it is a tough one. Your child needs to be comfortable speaking to adults that she may not know well, but must also be able to tell when *not* to speak to an adult. Stranger danger is an issue for all children, and yet when your child attends a new school or is just starting

a new school year, there will be new adults around her every day. Your child needs the confidence to speak to adults, even those she doesn't know, and the ability to recognize an adult that she should not speak to. Here are some stranger danger tips. The list is not exhaustive, but will get you started:

- *Do not help!* Adults you don't know don't ask children for help, children ask adults for help. If an adult asks your child for help, teach him to respond, "No, but I can get a grown-up to help you" and then to go get an adult right away.

- *Take a buddy!* It's important for your child to have a buddy with him when he goes places without you or when he is away from his teacher. Teach your child this from an early age.

- *Stay away from cars.* Tell your child never to go near a car that belongs to a stranger.

- *Use a password.* Give your child a password to be used in case there is an emergency and you need to send another person to pick up your child from school.

- *Answer questions.* Responding appropriately to questions from adults and other children is an important part of preschool and kindergarten. Teaching your child to respond to questions willingly and with enthusiasm will serve him well socially and academically.

Listening

Communication is not only about creating communication, or talking, it is also about receiving it, or listening. Your child needs to be able to listen, not just be quiet, but to truly listen. You can enhance your child's listening skills in several ways, such as:

1. *TV.* You know your child is watching the TV, but can she recall the details of what she hears? Ask her questions about the show. Watch nature shows together and talk about what you are seeing on TV as it happens ("Oh my gosh, is that a hippo? Wow!").

2. *Oral directions.* Give your child oral one-step directions such as, "Please bring the cup to me." When your child demonstrates an understanding of one-step directions, add a step. Examples of two-step directions are "Please wash your face and brush your teeth," or "Please put your clothes in the hamper and turn off the TV." The transition from one-step to two-step directions can be difficult so don't get discouraged.

Reading Readiness

Reading is an important skill in all grades, but it is the overriding benchmark by which preschoolers, kindergartners, and first graders are all judged. If your child is a struggling reader, it can affect the way you feel as a parent and your child's ability to progress in the grade level. It is a small consolation, but if your child has special needs, you should expect that he will struggle. The good news is that there are some things you can watch out for and support at home. Here are a few suggestions.

Reading Readiness Activities

Your child won't read until he or she is ready. Reading readiness activities will help her reach the developmental milestones she needs to reach before reading.

To complete the activities in this section, here is a list of recommended supplies:

- Books
- Sticky notes
- Paper
- Pencils, pens, colored markers
- Crayons

- Clothes to play dress-up

- Food coloring, uncooked pasta

Read to me! Your mission in these early years is to help your child love to read. The best way to create a love of reading is to read many stories together. Talk about the pictures that are in the book. With a familiar book, ask your child to "read" it to you by looking at the pictures and telling you what is happening in the story. Add some fun to retelling by asking your child to pick out some dress-up clothes that remind him of the main character or that are appropriate for the setting in the book. Pretend reading is an important reading readiness step. Play along when your child wants to read to you; you are helping your child with important skills!

Rhyme time. Say two words that rhyme. Ask your child if he notices anything about the words. If he says no, say the words again. If he still says no, ask him if the words sound the same or if they sound different. If he answers that they sound the same, say yes and explain that when words sound almost alike because they have the same ending sound, that is called a rhyme. If he says they sound different, say yes and ask which part of the word sounds different? Explain that when words sound alike except for the beginning sound, this is called a rhyme. Give your child more examples of rhyming words. Get a book with rhymes to read to your child. When your child begins to understand and identify rhymes, say one word and ask your child to tell you a word that rhymes with it. Ask your child to say a word and then you find a rhyming word.

It's all in a name. Buh, buh, buh Barbara. Say your child's name to her, emphasizing the first sound in her name, then say "Barbara starts with B." Ask your child if she can think of any more words that start with the same first sound (ball, baby, box, bark). Write a B and make the sound. Find something to eat that starts with B (bread). Paste colored pasta on construction paper in the shape of a B. Play with a toy that starts with B. Be creative and get the beginning letter in your child's name ingrained in her memory. Do the same thing for each subsequent letter in her name on consecutive days. Go from the beginning sound to the ending sound and then talk about the sounds in the middle.

Environmental Reading

Learning is foolproof when it comes naturally. Anything your child can learn from within her environment has a better chance of being retained than something that is learned out of context. In this section we will be looking at reading within your child's environment, in the form of signs that are posted all around and signs that you post.

Signs, signs everywhere are signs. Some of the first words your child will recognize and begin to read are signs. The first opportunities for your child to read are all around him in the form of signs. We read to learn, for entertainment, for directions, to know how to operate things (in the form of directions), and for safety (fire alarm, exit, danger). You want your child to know that signs are there to help him and you want your child to read them. Your street sign is a good example. Stop signs, store signs, school signs—there are many signs in our world. Fast-food restaurants and toy stores have signs that children can easily recognize (from the shape of the word and the color(s) of the sign). Encourage your child to "read" signs all over town. Recognizing the shapes of words and words in their environment is a prerequisite to reading books.

Post it. Once your child begins to recognize signs and words in his environment, add to the mix by posting signs of your own. The idea is to create a literacy-rich environment. You can do this by labeling the objects around your child. Label the door, the window, the toy box, the bed, and other things in your child's room. Trace the outline of the word (like you are going to cut it out) in a bright color to give your child a sense of the shape of the word and appeal to her visual sense like toy stores do. When your child starts to recognize some of the words you have posted around the room, take the sign down and paste it onto a piece of paper. Brainstorm related words (other words that start with the same letter, words that rhyme, or words that in some way "go with" the word on the sign) and list them on the paper for your child. Let your child draw pictures of some of the words you listed.

Writing Readiness

Writing readiness is the focus of preschool and kindergarten writing activities. Certainly children start writing numbers, letters, and their name during this time, but many kids are still preparing to learn to write. Here are some activities for writing readiness.

Writing Readiness Activities

To complete the activities in this section, here's a list of recommended supplies:

- Safety scissors
- Nontoxic glue or paste
- Dress-up clothes
- Paper
- Pencils (fat)
- Crayons
- Colored markers
- Chalk

Fine motor skills. If your child is having trouble writing her letters, there are several writing readiness activities that you can do to help her develop the motor skills she needs for writing.

1. *Cut and paste.* Any activity that involves cutting (with safety scissors) and pasting (with nontoxic glue or paste) is developing your child's fine motor skills by promoting the growth of the small muscles that are in his hand.

2. *Dress-up.* Playing dress-up with clothing that has small buttons, snaps, zippers, and laces is another sneaky way to develop the muscles and motor skills that your child needs.

Writing letters. This is a very important point: your child needs to make the proper motions to form letters. Once your child learns the wrong motion, it is one of the hardest things to correct that you will ever encounter. There are many methods for teaching kids how to print letters, but there are two components of the motion that never change (for printing):

1. *Start at the top.* The easiest way to make a straight line is to place your pencil at the top of the line and pull it down to the bottom. Kids with disabilities often start their letters by drawing a straight line from the bottom of the line and pushing up.

2. *Make the straight part first.* When writing a letter that has a straight part and a curved part, make the straight line first. The straight line tells you where to start and stop the curved line.

Writing letters doesn't have to be all about pencils and paper. Here are some fun ways to practice writing:

1. *Sand script.* Find a good spot of dirt or use a sandbox and grab a stick. Practice writing letters with a stick in the dirt or sand.

2. *Noodle letters.* Create letters using pasta colored with food coloring and glue (you can find the "recipe" at www.knowledgeessentials. com). Write some letters on the paper and ask your child to glue the pasta over your lines to make the letter.

3. *On my back.* Trace letters with your finger on your child's back. The first time, tell your child the letter and talk about the lines you are drawing. The next time just talk about the lines you are making and ask your child to tell you the letter. Let your child trace letters on your back for you to guess.

Math Readiness

Preschool and kindergarten math skills are pretty basic. We aren't looking for algebra here, just knowing about numbers and shapes.

Math Readiness Activities

To complete the activities in this section, here is a list of recommended supplies:

- Healthy, countable snacks; or colorful, tasty, countable snacks
- Big paper
- Colored markers
- Coins
- Poker chips
- Pencil
- Paper

Knows numbers. Your child may be having trouble telling the difference between numbers and letters. There is a number line and an alphabet strip in the classroom, and you have to read and write them, so it is understandable that a child can get confused. Your child may know the difference between a letter and a number but can't name and write either of them. If you have a child with special needs, you should help your child at home. You can try to

1. *Count snacks.* Counting the number of cookies in a package of minicookies, grapes, candies, chips, nuts, or anything that is countable and edible works here.

2. *Walk it off.* Count the number of steps it takes to get from one place to another. Count the steps from the couch to the TV, from the living room to the kitchen, from the car to the front door, and so on. Take it to the next level by keeping a chart of steps from the

Figure 8.1. Number Strip

same starting point to different places, such as a chart of your backyard in which you count the steps from the door to different things in your yard. Count the stairs as you walk up and down them. Start again each time you reach a landing.

3. *Slap It!* Using long paper (try a shopping bag that you cut down the sides and straighten out or two pieces of legal size paper taped together), make a number strip like the one above.

In this game you say a number and ask your child to put his hand over it as fast as he can, or ask him to slap the number and leave his hand on top of it so that you can see what he chose. Do this for several numbers and then trade places by letting your child call out the numbers and letting him decide if you chose the right one.

One-to-one correspondence. Once your child recognizes and says numbers, he needs to start learning what they stand for. Words are easy. To learn the word *chair*, you say the word while your child looks at a chair. Very concrete. Numbers aren't as easy because they can go with anything. Two chairs, one chair, ten chairs can also be two baseballs, one doll, and ten stickers. Once your child starts to read numbers, you have to immediately start making those numbers correspond with the same number of objects.

1. *Counting snacks.* Extend the activity in the previous section by writing down the numbers of all of the snacks that your child counted on a chart by snack type. You can find a chart to print at www.knowledgeessentials.com.

2. *Stack It!* Use the number strip that you made for *Slap It!* and loose change to teach your child how many objects each number stands

for. In this game tell your child that you are going to stack ten coins. Point to the number ten on the strip and then ask your child to place one coin in each square. After your child has placed the coins, ask her to put each coin that is on the strip on top of the number ten. Then point to the number nine. Tell your child that you are going to make a stack of nine coins by placing one coin in each square but stopping at the number nine. Ask your child to place each coin that is on the strip on top of the coin in the nine square. Do this for each number. When all of the stacks are in place, talk about their properties. Which stack is the tallest? Why? Which stack has the most coins? Which stack has the least? Why?

Shape it up! Your child will be using more shapes in art projects and starting to learn the names of shapes in preschool and kindergarten.

1. *I Spy.* Play the classic game with a learning twist and only choose things that have a geometric shape. "I spy something square and blue."

2. *It's in the Cards.* Using index cards, draw a circle on each card with obviously different sizes: extra small, small, medium, large, and extra large. Take the next five cards and draw five different sizes of triangles on them. Draw squares on the next five cards, using the same sizing scale, and rectangles on the next five cards. Use a different color marker for each shape (all circles are blue, squares are red, and so on). Shuffle the cards and give them to your child. Ask him to separate the cards into a different pile for each shape. Once he has sorted the cards, he should organize each pile from smallest to largest.

3. *Shaped!* Help your child find shapes in his environment. Ask your child to name the shape of a door, a window, or a clock face. Teaching him to notice shapes in his environment will help him learn the shapes very quickly.

Assessment

You want to monitor your child's progress at all times, but that can lead to inaccurate conclusions if you take it too seriously. What you may view as a serious setback may actually be a step toward a long-term goal, which is why you want to work with your child's teacher or other IEP team member when interpreting assessments. You can add valuable information about your child that will be considered when interpreting your child's short- and long-term assessments, and this section will steer you in the right direction.

Properly Observe Your Child's Skills

A common mistake is to forget to distinguish between skills that are slow in emerging and those that are different in quality, form, and function. There is a world of difference between a skill that is delayed and one that is disordered. These signs can have little or no impact on later development. However, they may be early warning signs of later and more significant problems. Watch for patterns of atypical behavior. Your observations can be useful in confirming delays and developing the interventions your child needs. When recording informal observations, make sure you include

- The dates and times when you observe the problem
- How long and how often the problem occurs
- What area of development is impacted
- The setting in which you observe the problem and the activity that your child is trying to do
- Does this problem affect interaction in play groups or with peers?

If you are concerned that your child is not developing at the same pace or in the same way as most other children, or if your child seems to be *losing* skills—in other words, starts to not be able to do the things they *could* do in the past—you should have a professional see them right away. Consult your primary care provider and discuss your concerns. The sooner you get a diagnosis, the sooner you can begin the appropriate treatment and the better the progress your child can make.

Daily Assessment

Definitely leave the daily assessment to your child's teacher, but we know you can't stop yourself from watching your child and making some fast judgments regarding how you view your child's progress or lack of it. Use Table 8.1 to get a feel for how you might consider reacting to what you observe.

Annual Assessment

If your child has already been identified as having special needs, you are probably intimately familiar with the word *assessment*. Assessment isn't all about medical or cognitive testing. Much of assessment, and much of the most reliable assessment, occurs through consistent and considered observation of your child. You are an important part of this component of assessment, so let's get you ready!

Your child will have annual assessments at school, and those results will be discussed and applied at your child's IEP meeting. You can really help the process by saving things throughout the school year that, when looked at as a whole, give extraordinary insight to your child and a context to the test scores. Some things you may want to save and analyze as a whole are

- Writing samples
- Reading log (list the books your child most likes to listen to and try to read)
- List of some favorite toys
- Artwork
- Photographs of your child alone and with friends and family
- Standardized test scores

Table 8.1. Sample Daily Assessments

Type of Observation	What you might see	What you will want to do	What you should consider doing instead
Behavior	Your child is stealing small things from the classroom.	Put child in time-out and tell him that stealing is wrong.	Explain that you know he likes the object, but if everyone took something home every day, soon there wouldn't be anything fun left at school.
Social interaction	Your child plays alone.	Tell your child to ask if she can play with the other kids.	When you catch your child involved in play, ask if you can play too. Ask how to play and follow her rules. Stay involved for five minutes and gradually work toward fifteen minutes. Model the behavior you hope to see.
Educational Performance	Cannot write the letters of his name.	Make your child trace the letters of his name.	Provide small manipulative toys, clay, lacing cards, markers, stickers, scissors, and so on. Write his name, and make sure that he can see your hand.
Classroom attitudes	Doesn't follow clean-up rules.	Emphasize to your child that she has to follow the rules.	Catch your child doing the right thing and compliment her. Say things like, "I like the way you are helping," or " I can tell you've learned the rule about_____."

- Teacher communication
- Your observation journal

Your child will go through the evaluation process described in Chapter One, and depending on your child's age, if your child is eligible, the next step will be to form an Individual Family Services Plan or an Individual Education Plan.

Being attentive to your child's special needs is the best thing you can do to help your child succeed. This includes

- Monitoring development
- Attending meetings
- Seeking opportunities for your child to be around children who do not have special needs
- Providing your physically disabled child with opportunities to be with other children who have similar disabilities
- Supplementing your child's education through learning moments at home
- Taking your child to physical, emotional, or occupational therapy appointments, and
- Taking your child to medical appointments and following all of the medical instructions exactly.

Elementary School

9

Elementary school carries big changes in physical and emotional development for all children, particularly when transitioning from half to full days at school, eating lunch at school, and being around children who are older than they are. It may also be the first time that you are able to notice that your special-needs child develops at a slower pace than others. Conversely, you may have been aware of your child's slower rate of development for years, and elementary school simply reinforces your desire to help your child attain on-grade-level achievement. In either case, simple at-home activities can significantly affect your child's development. This chapter will give you practical tips for helping your child learn at home and easy-to-use tools for assessing your child's progress. Let's start with some learning activities!

Building-Block Skills

Some basic skills affect your child's ability to learn in any subject area. This section uses the concept of color-coding to teach several core skills.

Color My World!

Using color as a visual cue for your child can help him develop many skills that may otherwise be difficult for a child with learning disabilities. To complete the activities in this section, here is a list of recommended supplies:

- Colored markers
- Colored labels
- Colored folders
- Colored notebooks
- Colored blocks or Legos™
- Calendar
- Paper
- Poster board
- Food coloring
- Pasta
- Colored beads
- Colored bins
- Marbles
- Paint

Teach Patterns

Patterns and sequences are the basis for reading, math, history, science, and just about any other subject you can think of. Identifying and continuing patterns with anything of color—colored blocks, Legos™, marbles, paint, crayons, or colored markers—helps your child recognize and continue patterns. Start with just two colors—red, blue, red, blue—by either stacking blocks or coloring stripes. Put the first couple of colors together and then ask your child, "What color goes next?" and let your child continue the pattern on his own. Add more colors to the pattern and mix it up—such as red, red, blue, red, red, blue—using more than one medium and more than one learning session to teach the skill. Use blocks one time and paint the next; try play dough or pasta dyed with food coloring to teach the skill. You can find directions for making your own play dough and the recipe for dyeing pasta at www.knowledgeessentials.com.

Mastering patterns is a skill that will help your child with early reading and math, in particular. After all, multiplication is a pattern. Phonics is based on the patterns of letters and the sounds they make. Understanding patterns is a skill that your child will build on throughout her education.

Teach Sequencing

Teaching your early learner about sequence is very similar to teaching about patterns and is easily and effectively done through colors. This is particularly effective with a child who has special learning needs because it doesn't entail recognizing all of the numbers or letters. You teach sequencing the same way that you teach patterns, except you label the patterns "A-B patterns or 1-2 patterns." As you lay down a red block, it will be "A" and when you lay down a blue block it will be "B." You have now made an "A-B pattern" using color cues that your child can associate with hearing the letter, the sequence of the letters in the alphabet, and a familiar pattern (alphabet) that extends the skill closer to her early reading and math skills. A "1-2 pattern" is the same as an "A-B pattern"; you simply substitute the numbers for the letters.

The next step in the process is to use colors to write the letters and numbers and place them in the same patterns and sequences.

Provide Visual Cues

Working on patterns and sequences with colors makes it easy to associate those colors with a particular letter or number, which can be one of the first visual cues your child uses when learning his letters and numbers.

Color as a visual cue is something that probably began with the McDonald's golden arches. Traffic signals, traffic signs, corporate logos, sports teams, and the car you ride in are all early visual color cues for your child. You began transferring those cues to learning reading and math in the previous two sections, and now we are identifying ways to extend color cues with your child's needs to assist her in attaining more skills. Here are some ways you can use color:

1. *Letters and numbers.* Try writing all of the vowels in one color and all of the consonants in another color in an "alphabet strip" and leave it hanging in your child's room until she can identify, say, and write the letters. You can also write all of the even numbers in one color and all of the odd numbers in another color. As your child masters numbers, extend the pattern to three colors for three numbers, then four, and so on. You will be reinforcing patterns and sequences at the same time that you are working on numbers. Color patterns are a great way to lay the groundwork for multiplication tables.

2. *Days of the week.* Start with a whiteboard and divide it into seven strips to make a weekly calendar (you can use paper, too, and you can print out a weekly calendar at www.knowledgeessentials.com) and then write all of the weekdays in one color and the weekend days in another color. Once your child masters weekdays and weekends, add another color by labeling a day of the week when your child has a different activity in a different color—or just label Wednesday in another color since it is mid-week.

3. *School subjects.* You can help your child understand that there are distinct subject areas at school and keep his work together by color-coding parts of his notebook with colored markers or labels or buying notebooks of certain colors for each subject. The organizational aspects of this activity will bear fruit as your child enters the later stages of elementary school.

4. *Behavioral cues.* It is easy to talk about stoplights and what the colors mean and then use those colors to cue your child's behavior. You can say "red light" when your child needs to stop doing something, "yellow light" when your child is getting close to the line (that you don't want him to cross), and "green light" when giving permission for her to do something. You can also write all chores in one color and rewards in another color.

5. *Organizational skills.* As your child begins to utilize color cues in learning activities, it will be natural to extend their use to reinforce organizational skills. Color-code your child's room, such as using a blue bin for books and a red bin for cars and dolls, and so on. Most learning-disabled children have a lot of trouble with organization, and building those skills early can make a significant difference in your child's ability to organize learning concepts.

Reading Skills

Special-needs children may experience problems with reading skills that will affect all other areas of learning.

To complete the activities in this section, here is a list of recommended supplies:

- Paper
- Colored pencils
- Pencils
- Colored markers
- Chart paper
- Big paper
- Stickers to put on chart
- Books
- Index cards

Reading Activities

Blends

A certain amount of learning to read is simple memorization. Your child must learn to recognize letters, know how they sound, know how letters sound when next to each other, know what word the letters make when together, and what the word means. A common stumbling block for struggling readers is not knowing how to make the transition from single letter sounds to blended letter sounds. Blended letter sounds are a stepping-stone to being able to sound out and spell words.

There are many activities for helping your child with blends; this is a simple one that is easy to do.

Blending Chart

You can help your child work on blends at home by making charts such as this for your child to fill in with words that are appropriate.

_____AT	_____IT	_____ET
_____AT	_____IT	_____ET
_____AT	_____IT	_____ET
_____AT	_____IT	_____ET
_____AT	_____IT	_____ET
_____AT	_____IT	_____ET
_____ED	_____OP	_____UN
_____ED	_____OP	_____UN
_____ED	_____OP	_____UN
_____ED	_____OP	_____UN
_____ED	_____OP	_____UN
_____ED	_____OP	_____UN
ST_____	TH_____	CL_____
ST_____	TH_____	CL_____
ST_____	TH_____	CL_____
ST_____	TH_____	CL_____
ST_____	TH_____	CL_____

ST_____	TH_____	CL_____
TR_____	SH_____	PL_____
TR_____	SH_____	PL_____
TR_____	SH_____	PL_____
TR_____	SH_____	PL_____
TR_____	SH_____	PL_____
TR_____	SH_____	PL_____

Place any letters on the chart that your child needs to work with. You can also make flashcards with just a blend and a line either before it (for words that end in the blend), after it (for words that start with the blend), or on both sides (for words with a blend in the middle of the word).

Tip: Try color-coding the blends!

Word Categories

Students from kindergarten to third grade are working on "sight words," or words that your child should know without sounding them out. You can find a list of these by grade level at www.knowledgeessentials.com. Students with special needs have trouble memorizing sight words. A trick that will help your child is to categorize the words (and perhaps color-code them) so that your child has a context for the words and can associate them with other words in the category. Some examples of word categories are

Action: pick, put, pull, buy, carry, open, use, show, start, stop, wash

Away: away, down, far, out, there, from

Connecting: because, but, and, with, too

Feeling: want, hurt, kind, laugh, thank, wish, like, funny

Little: if, of, or, so, to, as, for, the

Number: one, two, three, four, five, six, seven, eight, nine, ten

Question: who, which, where, why, how, can, may, what, when, could, would, shall

Sharing: let, gave, give, get, bring, take, help, together

Temperature: cold, warm, hot

Amount: a, all, an, both, every, many, much, some, the, only, just, any

Be: be, am, are, been, is, was, were

Do: do, did, does, done, make, made, try, must, will, sleep, sit

Good: fast, best, better, clean, yes, good, pretty, well, very, please, new

Moving: came, come, play, jump, go, goes, ran, going, run, walk, ride, fly, went, fall

Other people: he, him, she, his, their, them, they, you, your

School: draw, know, word, write, sing, read, think

Size: round, big, light, little, long, small

When: before, after, once, again, old, soon, first, about, always, then, today, now

Anything: that, it, this, these, its, those

Color: black, blue, brown, green, red, white, yellow

Eating: ate, cut, drink, eat, full

Life: live, see, look, saw, grow

No: don't, never, no, not

Possession: had, found, got, has, have, hold, keep, own, find

Self: I, me, myself, our, we, us

Talk: call, say, tell, said, ask

Where: at, around, by, in, into, on, over, right, under, up, upon, here, off

Make a chart with these words and color-code them; then make flash cards with the words written in the color that matches the chart. Use the flash cards for drilling your child, but also use them to make up your own games—such as a memory game where your child chooses pairs of words that are in the same category instead of having two of the same word make a pair.

Chunking

If your child is reading words but is having trouble reading new sentences in a natural voice, practice new sentences with your child and use a method called "chunking." Chunking a sentence means reading the sentence in parts instead of trying to read it all at once. An example:

New Sentence:

By the end of November the bears had returned to their caves where they were getting ready for a long winter's rest.

New Sentence "Chunked":

By the end of November / the bears had returned to their caves / where they were getting ready / for a long winter's rest.

As your child progresses, increase the size of the chunks until he is reading the whole sentence without hesitation.

Repeated Reading

Even when your child is comfortable reading new sentences, her reading rate may still need improvement. This is a tried-and-true activity for increasing your child's fluency and speed:

1. Choose a fairly comfortable, interesting selection to practice reading. It should be too long to memorize: one hundred or so words for younger children, two hundred or more words for older ones.
2. Monitor the word recognition level of the passages. On the first reading, your child should read with 85 percent accuracy or better before starting practice; otherwise, the passage is too hard.

3. Prepare a chart for your child.

4. Time his first unrehearsed oral reading passage. Mark the chart for Timed Reading 1.

5. Let your child practice the passage aloud as many times as possible for the next day or two.

6. Time the reading again, mark the chart for Timed Reading 2, and show your child how to mark her own chart.

7. Continue timing at intervals of several days. As the rate increases for the first passage, help your child set a new rate goal.

8. When your child reaches the goal, begin a new passage of equal (not greater) difficulty. Successive portions of a long story are perfect. Repeat steps 3 through 6.

9. Keep the practice passages at the same level of difficulty until an acceptable rate of speed and accuracy (that you should set in partnership with your child's teacher) is reached on the first or second reading, then move on to harder passages.

Those were just a few ideas to help your child increase his reading skills. Take the ideas and extend them in ways that reflect your own creativity, your child's interests, and her teacher's suggestions.

Writing Skills

Writing is a complex skill for any child to learn, and students with special needs are no different. You start with having to physically form the letters; know how to spell the words you want to write; form technically correct sentences, paragraphs, and eventually essays—and you need to do it with style. Writing is a conduit for self-expression, and it is one of the most common areas affected by learning disabilities. This section will show you some ways to reinforce what your child is learning in school through opportunities to practice with you, at home, in a focused and nonthreatening environment.

To complete the activities in this section, here is a list of recommended supplies:

- Pencils (standard and large size)
- Colored pencils
- Handwriting paper
- Colored paper
- Notebooks
- Journal
- Computer
- Scissors
- Glue
- Index cards
- Large sheets of paper or poster board
- Jacks

Writing Activities

Environmental Writing

Your child won't want to feel like he has to sit down and work on the great American novel every day after school—and even writing a paragraph can feel like that to a ten-year-old. Instead of writing for the sake of writing, incorporate it into your child's day. Some examples are:

Journal. Keeping a daily or weekly journal is an easy way to build writing skills while freely and creatively expressing thoughts. Some kids may find it hard to start a journal; you can help your child out by brainstorming reasons that he might like to keep a journal (expressing private thoughts, looking back at it when he gets older, and so forth) and things he might like to write about (anything you two can think of). Your child may find it more intriguing to keep an electronic journal if you have a computer that he can use.

Scrapbooks. Scrapbooking is a great activity for kids with special needs because it involves taking items your child finds special and presenting them in a creative way. When you add writing a sentence or a paragraph about each item in the scrapbook it is an activity that reinforces writing skills in a fun way.

Thank-You Notes. It's never too early to write thank-you notes, and it is an easy way to work on handwriting and forming a short paragraph. Talk to your child about what she wants to thank the recipient for and how she wants to say it. Talk about how to best express her thoughts by deciding what to write first, second, and then third. Make sure your child addresses the envelope too! Draw an example envelope on a piece of paper with the address and return address properly written on it for your child to look at while she is addressing the envelope.

E-Mail. Letting your child send an e-mail that you read prior to it being sent (to a person who you know and permit your child to e-mail) is a form of written communication that entails proper grammar, sentence structure, and well-formed written ideas. Helping your child send an e-mail is a perfectly innocuous way to incorporate more writing into your child's day.

Letters. Writing a letter is a fun way to practice writing skills. Pick up some attractive stationery to let your child use for letter writing. Help your child with the format of the letter, starting with one sentence and working your way up to a multiparagraph letter with the proper salutation.

Holiday Cards. Making holiday cards and writing a message inside them is a fun activity that reinforces writing skills. Take this as an opportunity to talk about the things that symbolize the holiday that your child is making the card for. Brainstorm a theme for the card, relating your child's written message to the way she is going to decorate the card. This is also a fun activity for using skills such as:

- Rhyming
- Synonyms
- Antonyms
- Alliteration

Stories. The next time Mother's Day or Father's Day rolls around, ask your child to write a story instead of buying a gift. It will be a good opportunity to motivate your child to write something creative and lengthy without feeling like he is doing homework. You can help your child with the writing process by printing out the writing web you will find at www.knowledgeessentials.com. Make sure the story is illustrated!

Structural Skills

Forming a proper sentence with the correct parts of speech and punctuation is difficult for many kids. Punctuation can be difficult for special-needs students, and a common classroom adjustment is to allow students to submit work with little to no punctuation. If your child has ADHD, written expression with proper punctuation can be particularly difficult. There are many worksheets on the Internet that list sentences without punctuation, so your child can fill in the punctuation. The challenge is to help your child use punctuation properly and understand the nuances that punctuation can bring to the same set of words. An idea that you may want to try is to make flash cards with these punctuation marks on them:

- Apostrophe
- Parentheses
- Comma
- Italics
- Quotation marks

- Colon

- Semicolon

- Period

- Exclamation point

- Question mark

Capitalization   Using a large sheet of paper, write a sentence on the paper without punctuation and then ask your child to place the card with the proper punctuation marks where they go in the sentence. Ask your child to read the sentence aloud with that punctuation. Ask your child to put a different kind of punctuation in the same sentence. Did it make sense? Sometimes it does and sometimes it doesn't. Talk with your child about the way punctuation changes the sentence's meaning.

Handwriting   You and your child have probably been working on fine motor skills since she was a small child, and it's important to continue doing so. After your child learns to write—which is the goal for younger children when working on fine motor skills—cursive writing is introduced almost immediately, and your child has to master a second way of writing. Activities that develop fine motor skills are important parts of helping your child develop good handwriting. Try things such as:

- Working with clay and play dough to increase muscle strength in your child's hands

- Doing puzzles (with increasingly smaller pieces)

- Playing jacks

- Art projects that involve cutting, gluing, drawing on, and tearing paper

- Playing with games, blocks, cars, and other things with small pieces

- Buttoning clothes, lacing and tying shoe laces, and using zippers

Practice makes perfect. It doesn't seem fun, but a lot of handwriting is practicing it until your child masters it. Your mission is to give your child the tools that make it easer and make practicing handwriting as fun as possible. Try such things as:

- Using handwriting paper (you can print it out at www.knowledge essentials.com)
- Incorporating colors into writing by using colored paper and colored pencils or pens
- Finding fun reasons to write
- Charting progress
- Rewarding efforts

Math Skills

The skills and strategies needed for successful mathematical problem solving develop from the preschool years, when children develop an understanding of the base-10 numerical system. During these early years, they typically develop the "number sense" needed to process and manipulate numerical information. In primary school, children continue to acquire mathematical knowledge and skills and are exposed to a variety of math problems requiring addition and subtraction operations. Like many special-needs kids, your child may need to further develop his sense of the base-10 number system before he can fully grasp problem-solving activities.

To complete the activities in this section, here is a list of recommended supplies:

- Countable snacks
- Coins
- Poker chips
- Paper plates

- Brads
- Colored markers
- Calendar
- Paper
- Pencils
- Large sheets of paper or poster board

Math Activities

Number Sense

Grouping. You and your child can group almost anything by 10s. Count out 10 grapes to eat for a snack, stack clothes you fold together in stacks of 5 or 10, group toys by 10s and so on.

Coins. Group and stack coins by 10s. Count the 10s to make a full roll of coins, and then roll them.

Skip counting. Count by 10s instead of 1s. When your child can count by 10s past 100, switch to counting by 5s and 2s.

It's About Time!

Learning to tell and manage time can be difficult for students with disabilities, but mastery of time is critical to success. School success stems from the proper perception and use of time during individual class times, throughout the day, and over extended periods of time. Laying the foundation for time management when your child is young will give her the head start she needs for managing increasing demands on her time as she gets older.

Timers. Much of life is about meeting deadlines, particularly school. Both high and low learners waste time. Reinforcing time management can be as simple as asking your child to choose what he or she wants for lunch within sixty seconds or less. It's hard for small children to answer questions in a finite time period. Help them learn how by playing games that use timers for short tasks.

Clocks. Your child needs to be able to tell time on digital and traditional clocks. If your child is having a hard time with numbers or understanding how a clock face is divided, try making your own clocks on paper plates that are color-coded by the hour. Start by drawing a clock that color-codes the numbers. You can make your own dials that move by cutting hands out of another paper plate and pinning them to your clock face with a brad. You can also draw different clocks with hands that are drawn on and then color-code sections of the clocks to help indicate the time.

Estimation. Your child may have difficulty developing a proper concept of time. Everyone has to work on this, but kids with special needs usually need extra help. It's easy to help develop this skill by asking your child simple questions when you are going about your day together, such as, "How long do you think it will take to put the dishes away?" or "Guess how long we'll be in the grocery store." Ask your child to time the activity and you are reinforcing telling time as well.

Seasons. Knowing the seasons of the year, how long they last, and the order in which they come is integral to your child's overall concept of time. It is also basic to helping your child learn how to take care of herself, such as knowing how to appropriately dress for the weather. It is hard to understand seasons when you just talk about them. You need a calendar that has all twelve months of the year on one page. Color-code it and leave it in plain sight all year; you can even make an X over the months and seasons as they pass. Another good activity is to get a piece of large paper or poster board and divide it into twelve squares. Write the name of the month at the top of each square, and ask your child to draw a picture in each square that shows something about that month or season.

Weekly calendar. Time concepts are dependent on mastering the days of the week. Weekly calendars are easy ways to color-code days that are particularly busy, days with special activities, and days when your child may have sports practice or tutoring. Every parent and every child needs to be cautious of over-scheduling, and having a master weekly calendar helps you remember how many things are already in your week and helps your child develop a sense of how much can be done in one week.

Problem Solving

Many students in kindergarten through third grade, especially students with learning disabilities, have difficulty learning how to solve math word problems because they can't remember and apply the steps it takes to solve one. The following are examples of second- and third-grade problems:

- Susan has 10 stickers. Her friend Tony gave her 6 more stickers. How many stickers does Susan have altogether?

- Steve has 14 marbles. Amy has 5 marbles. How many more marbles does Steve have?

Textbooks give your child a four-step process: (1) read the problem, (2) decide what to do, (3) compute, and (4) check your answer. "Read" the problem for understanding is the first step, and that involves understanding the relationship between numbers, words, and symbols in the problem (number sense skills). Your child's number sense provides the basis for deciding what to do to solve the problem. Most students acquire the skills and strategies needed to "read the problem" and "decide what to do" to solve it in kindergarten and first grade. Many students with learning disabilities do not pick up these skills and strategies then, and they need extra help to solve math problems before they gain the strategies to solve the problems in their math textbooks and in their daily lives.

Let's use the four-step process as the basis for working on problem solving at home.

1. *Read the problem.* Talk about math in daily life by discussing out loud how you think about math problems that you have to figure out every day. "There are four of us eating dinner together and this frozen lasagna serves six. Will we have enough? How much of it will be left over?" Our family drinks five bottles of water a day during sports practice. Water comes in packs of twelve. How many packs do we need to buy to last one week?" "This costs $10 and I have $7. How much more money do I need?" You get the idea. You set up problems every day in normal life. Say them aloud as you run into them so that your child is able to put math problems in context while listening to a problem and learning how to set it up to be solved.

Don't forget your number sense activities here too. Your child needs to have that as a solid basis to begin working with numbers and symbols.

2. *Set it up!* What do you do if your child is getting hung up on the transition of identifying a math problem and deciding how to solve it? Your child probably understands numbers well and can take groups of objects—or manipulatives—and add or subtract them, which means she is having trouble with the language of math and math symbols. Flash cards are the best standby teaching tool of all time. Make flash cards for the symbols. Start with just the plus sign, minus sign, and equals sign. Next, grab some blocks, candies, marbles, or anything your child can add or subtract. Ask your child to make two groups of the items (three and five items, two and seven items, and so forth). Say the problem aloud like you did in step one, and then ask your child to place the flash card between the groups that show what needs to happen to solve the problem. Ask your child to place the equals sign by the groups and continue on to computing the problem.

Next, transfer the activity from the manipulatives to the paper by letting your child draw something that stands for the objects. For example, for a problem in which you need to add 5 and 3, draw a picture like the one in Figure 9.1 to help your child set up the problem.

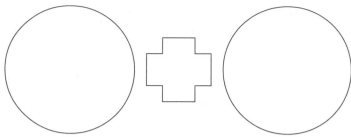

Figure 9.1.

Let your child draw five X's or anything she wants in one circle and three X's or anything else in the other circle. Use colored paper, colored pencils, and other fun things to set up the problem. Next, ask your child to write the number underneath the circle.

Both of these activities should be extended to computing the problem.

3. *Compute.* Computing the problem is often less difficult for students with disabilities than setting the problem up. Computation is concrete, and your child can use manipulatives to help him visualize the problem. Many IEPs even allow calculators as a modification because computation is viewed as less important than being able to identify a math problem and conceptualize the steps involved in solving it.

4. *Check your work.* This is a great step, and you want to teach your child to do it, but it is less important than steps one and two when your child is young. Talk to your child about how to do it and model it for her. Money is a great way to show your child the importance of checking your math calculations and is a very concrete example. If something cost $5 and you gave the clerk $20, how much change should you get? How do you know it is the right amount of change?

There are many ways to reinforce math concepts throughout the day and lots of fun and creative ways to reinforce them at home. Take the suggestions in this chapter and use them as the basis for making your own activities. Let your imagination run free and keep your child's interests in mind.

Assessment

Like every parent, you want to keep track of your child's progress. As a parent of a child with special needs you probably have more understanding of your child's skills than most parents. The IEP process alone gives you great insight for monitoring progress because it identifies your child's baseline skill sets and sets reasonable goals to achieve during the school year. Use that information as the great tool that it is.

Daily Assessment

Knee jerk reactions are hard to resist, so let Table 9.1 help you knowledgeably interpret your assessments.

Table 9.1.   Sample Daily Assessments

Type of Assessment	What you might see	What you will want to do	What you should consider doing instead
Behavior	Your child has a bad attitude, does not easily cooperate, or is disruptive during class.	Discipline your child for his behavior or separate him from the group.	Identify her strengths and work together to make a list of more positive things she can say or do when responding to other students or a class activity.
Social interaction	Your child has very few friends and doesn't seem to want to make any.	Encourage her to take the initiative when around others, but allow her to be alone when she wants—or even worse, tell her sad stories of cliques that were mean when you were a child.	Work with the school counselor to plan ways to teach him specific social skills.

(continued)

Table 9.1. Sample Daily Assessments *(continued)*

Type of Assessment	What you might see	What you will want to do	What you should consider doing instead
Educational performance	Your child's schoolwork is okay, but you have to constantly supervise him to get it there.	Hire a tutor to watch him.	Work with her teacher to create step-by-step assignments that she can do on her own. Build in a small reward system (such as stars on a chart) for each step completed.
Classroom attitudes	Your child never volunteers answers and is reluctant to participate in group activities.	Carefully manipulate environments and activities so that your child can be alone.	Work with your child's teacher to understand upcoming curriculum so that you can work with him on content to be covered and plan specific things for him to contribute.

Annual Assessment

Your child will have annual assessments at school, and those results will be discussed and applied at your child's IEP meeting. You can really help the process by saving things throughout the school year that, when looked at as a whole, give extraordinary insight to your child and a context to the test scores. Some things you want to save and analyze as a whole are

- Writing samples
- Reading log (dated list of books your child has read)
- Vocabulary journal (try generating from spelling word lists)
- Examples of math assignments
- Artwork
- Letters to friends and family

- Photographs of your child alone and with friends and family (in order to gauge body language when your child is alone versus in a group)
- Child's journal
- Weekly calendars
- Unit and lesson tests from that school year
- Standardized test scores
- Teacher communication

Middle School 10

Middle school is another one of those watershed moments for you and your child. Transitioning from elementary school can be difficult for children with special needs. It may be the first time your child is changing classes. Your child will have more teachers throughout the school day than in elementary school, and your child will become a teenager during middle school. Puberty begins and your child really starts to grow up. Middle school is also the time you start to plan for your child's exit from special services. Even if he will be receiving special services through high school, by eighth grade it will be time to start thinking about what your child's daily life will look like after public school so that the next four years can be spent preparing her to be successful in her post-school endeavors. Let's start by just dealing with the present: starting middle school!

Transitioning from Elementary School to Middle School

Middle school is usually the first time that students have changed classrooms for different classes. Developmentally, there is a huge difference between a sixth grader and an eighth grader, and it is very intimidating for a sixth grader to go to middle school with the older children. Think of this as kindergarten for your 'tween. They are new to the school, new to the schedule, and there is a big difference between them and their older classmates. The transition from elementary to middle school may be even more dramatic for your special-needs child if school personnel do not provide assistance and implement a transition plan.

Since this is such a big transition, let's take a look at what happens to students without disabilities during this pivotal moment. During the transition from elementary school to middle school children can experience a decline in

- Self perception
- Social performance, and
- Academic performance, including a decline in grade-point average.

The declines are normally gradual and temporary. You should be concerned if they are either dramatic or sustained.

These declines can be directly related to transitioning to middle school or to just plain old teen angst. Either answer is logical and acceptable, but the fact is that the declines happen and as parents you must expect at least temporary declines and be prepared to deal with them. As special-needs parents, don't be surprised if your child takes the changes associated with middle school particularly hard.

Building-Block Skills

There are basic skills that middle schoolers need to be successful, and your special-needs child is no different. Time management, and consequently homework management, is challenging during adolescence, so we are concentrating on those issues in this section.

To complete the activities in this section, here is a list of recommended supplies:

- Day planner
- Kitchen timer
- Homework supplies, such as:
  - Pens
  - Paper
  - Pencils
  - Erasers
  - Computer
- A quiet, well-lit area

Time the Avenger

Time management is so critical for students with disabilities that we have been talking about it in each section of the book. The most common regular classroom adjustment for students with special needs is extending time allotments for classroom assignments and testing. Your child will need help mastering time management even if the mastery occurred in an earlier grade. Each year your child is in school, time requirements adjust because your child is expected to fit more work into less time as he gets older. Consistently working on time management at home will be a component of success in school. Appropriate time-management tools and activities include the following:

Day planner. A day planner is a great tool for students with disabilities who change classes. Ask your child to write her daily schedule in her day planner. Help your child remember to take it with her to school by including an assignment sheet in the back of the planner.

Assignment sheets. Make a grid on a sheet of paper with your child's daily class schedule in one column, his daily homework assignments

Table 10.1. Daily Assignment Sheet

Class	Homework	Teacher's Initials
English/Language Arts		
Math		
Social Studies		
Science		
Health (or other elective course)		
Home Economics (or other elective course)		

in a second column, and a spot for your child's teacher's initials in the third column. It will look something like Table 10.1.

Your child will be responsible for filling in her homework assignments for each class and then asking the teacher to initial that the homework assignment is listed correctly or that there is no homework that day. It is your responsibility to ask to see the assignment sheet each day and help your child make the time to complete her homework. You can find a daily assignment sheet to print out at www.knowledgeessentials.com.

School schedule. Your child may have trouble getting used to his school schedule. Transitioning from the self-contained classroom in elementary school to changing classrooms for each subject or course is difficult for every child, but your special-needs child may need extra help staying organized and adjusting to a new schedule. With the physical changes of moving from class to class, your child can easily experience setbacks because he has a new teacher in each class. Your child's special-needs teacher is there to give your child the consistency associated with their "homeroom teacher" of elementary school, but it is still a hard adjustment for your child to make. Giving her a concrete view of her daily schedule—easily listed in her day planner—will comfort your child and restore some needed confidence.

Timers. Your child has just started changing classes in a certain amount of time, and it is really hard to manage going to the bathroom, going to her locker, visiting with her friends, and getting to class all in a three- to five- minute passing period. You can help your child by asking him to do a finite task, such as setting the table, and setting the kitchen timer for three minutes as the allotted time period for this task. Don't let your child race through the task carelessly; the point is to show him that efficient use of time allows him to effectively achieve certain tasks. Activities such as this give your child a sense of time.

Homework

Middle school and high school are all about homework. You want to help your child with homework, but you are unsure about how to do it because it's been so long since you studied trigonometry and the Revolutionary War. You don't have to know the subject areas enough to be able to help your child. Here are ten tips to help with homework:

1. *Keep in touch with your child's teachers to be fully aware of the quantity and the quality of the homework turned in.* You can even add a column to your child's daily homework sheet for the teacher to initial that all previous homework has been turned in.

2. *Set a schedule, including both a beginning and an ending time.* Most kids need some time to unwind after school before they tackle their homework, but you risk having a sleepy child if homework time is too close to bedtime. If your child has homework to do over the weekend, help your child develop the habit of completing it on Friday night or Saturday morning. Sunday night homework can create a sense of panic or stress if your child didn't leave enough time to complete it all.

3. *Encourage your child to divide the homework assignment into "What I can do myself" and "What I need help with."* You should help only with that part of the homework your child cannot do independently, such as using flash cards, practicing spelling tests, and clarifying assignments.

4. *Hold off on watching TV and other fun activities until homework is completed.* And don't fall for the multitasking approach: "I *need* to watch TV and do my homework together; this TV show is *part* of my homework."

5. *Provide a home study center for your child with adequate light and few distractions.* If your child concentrates better with "white noise" (music), provide that help. Also, a dictionary, paper, pens, computer, and so on, should be readily available.

6. *Use direct praise for doing the homework and even more for accomplishment.* "You've spelled eighteen out of twenty words correctly—that's the best you've done this semester!"

7. *Be available when your child is doing homework, so that you can answer a question if there is confusion.* If possible, it is better for you to be in another room, so you are easily accessible and yet not a distraction.

8. *Look over the homework when it is completed.* Do not correct it unless you have checked with the teacher. Seeing the pattern of errors is often helpful to a teacher.

9. *Daylight-homework-savings time should be implemented year-round when it comes to homework.* Maybe it is an "old wives' tale" or maybe it's a great trick played on me by my high school chemistry teacher, but it has been engrained into my psyche that you retain more when you study in the daylight.

10. *Allow bathroom, drink, or snack breaks (and set the timer), but insist on the completion of tasks.*

Reading Skills

Middle school is not too late to close your child's literacy gap, and here are some learning ideas to help.

To complete the activities in this section, here's a list of recommended supplies:

- Reading materials (newspapers, magazines, books, and so on)
- Dictionary
- Index cards
- Pens/colored markers
- Highlighters
- Paper
- Pencil

Reading-Skills Activities

Bad Company

Bad attitude: Your child's. Improving adolescents' literacy skills is more difficult than improving children's literacy skills, for a number of reasons. One major reason is attitude. Many middle schoolers have developed bad attitudes about reading, writing, and the whole subject of dealing with improving their academic skills—and understandably so, if they've been struggling with literacy for a while. There's no simple solution here. But it's important that whatever approach you use, you are in partnership with your child. She must understand that improving her reading and writing skills is not something that you are doing to her, but that it is something that is done with her. You and your child need to forge a partnership so that she understands the specifics of her skill gaps, what you both can do about it, and how long it will take. She also needs to understand the benefit she will gain from increasing her skills (such as completing homework faster, moving to another class where some of her friends may be, reducing adjustments to assignments so that she is doing work at the same pace as her friends, and other benefits) and can set realistic goals.

Bad attitude: Yours. It is easy to focus on the IEP and the accommodations and modifications that are associated with "evening the playing field" when it comes to your child's reading level. I've seen it happen: parents and students act as if they have given up and are saying, "You know what? You'll always read at, say, a third- or fourth-grade level. There's nothing we can do about that. So we're just going to focus on giving you books on tape, advanced organizers, and other things to accommodate your reading difficulty." And there's no longer a focus on closing that literacy gap or accelerating literacy skills. If you have fallen into that rut, break the cycle now. Your own actions and habits can affect your child's reading and learning attitude. Model reading skills and habits by reading often in front of your child by:

- Keeping a book handy (and reading it)
- Reading the newspaper each day and discussing something interesting from it with your child
- Looking things up on the Internet that you are interested in and reading the information that you find
- Reading labels at the grocery store and commenting on the nutritional value of the food you are considering buying
- Researching information about a type of car that your child is daydreaming he will get for his sixteenth birthday and then reading and commenting on car-specific information with him
- Anything else you can think of that demonstrates your reading habits and reasons that you read in daily life

Your child has not reached his peak learning potential at age thirteen, and you need to continue working with him to gain as many skills as possible throughout his life.

Vocabulary

Vocabulary knowledge is not something that can ever be fully mastered; it is something that expands and deepens over the course of a lifetime. Instruction in vocabulary involves far more than looking up words in a dictionary and using the words in a sentence. Vocabulary is acquired through indirect exposure to words and intentionally through explicit instruction in specific words and word-learning strategies. You should take your child's textbooks and make flash cards for the new words or look up new words regularly. Direct instruction in vocabulary is essential for students with special needs. In this activity, we are going to focus on some skills that give your child strategies for identifying the meanings of new words.

1. *Prefixes and suffixes* are letter groups that we add to the beginnings and endings of root words to change their meanings. Write a prefix on a piece of paper with a line after the prefix where the root word would go. Do the same thing for a suffix, but place the line where the word goes before the suffix.

Prefix	Suffix
un-	-ful
re-	-ness
in-	-less
dis-	-ly
non-	-ed
de-	-ing

Set your kitchen timer for two minutes and ask your child to brainstorm as many words as possible that can follow the prefix and write them down (you can write them down for your child as she says them aloud if she has trouble writing). Set your kitchen timer for another two minutes and ask your child to brainstorm all of the words that can go with the suffix.

Next, hand your child a newspaper or magazine and a highlighter. Ask your child to highlight all of the words he can find from his lists in the newspaper.

2. *Idioms* are phrases or expressions in which the entire meaning is different from the usual meanings of the individual words within the expression. Examples:

Raining cats and dogs

In the doghouse

Let sleeping dogs lie

Let the cat out of the bag

Has the cat got your tongue?

Hold your horses

Look a gift horse in the mouth

Eat like a horse

Hear it straight from the horse's mouth

Put the cart before the horse

Change horses in midstream

The straw that broke the camel's back

Have a cow

Until the cows come home

Ants in your pants

Take the bull by the horns

In a fine kettle of fish

Live high on the hog

Idioms are expressions that play on words to get an idea across to the reader or listener and that make wordplay the perfect way to teach your child about idioms or practice them. Here are some wordplay practice ideas:

1. Make up your own idioms, define them, and draw a picture that illustrates their meaning.

2. Use idioms as much as possible for an hour.

3. How many idioms can you use in one sentence? Don't have a cow; this game won't be the straw that breaks the camel's back.

4. How many sentences can you make from one idiom?

Writing Skills

Writing skills are important in every school subject. Writing allows your child to communicate answers to questions; form, develop, and express ideas; and be an avenue of self-expression for thoughts and ideas that may otherwise be too difficult for your child to communicate verbally. Still, writing skills can be tough to master. We are going to work on two strategies for writing in this section. In order to complete the activities in this section, here is a list of recommended supplies:

- Paper
- Pencils
- Notebooks
- Folders

Writing Skills Activities

The purpose of this section, unlike some others, is to teach you, as a parent, strategies to help your child get through his homework. The older your child gets, the more you will need to work with him on strategies for completing school assignments rather than adding more and more onto his plate through at-home learning activities.

Chunking

There is nothing worse than leaving a five-page writing assignment in the hands of a seventh grader who has no clue what it will take to complete the task. Chunking, a computer term meaning "bundles of information," refers to the strategy of breaking information or a task into smaller manageable parts. This is an important strategy for all students.

As parents, we can help our children appreciate these important aspects about the chunking process:

- We store and organize information more efficiently in small chunks
- Everything begins with one small step
- The small steps then lead up to a bigger accomplishment

Power

When dealing with writing, chunking is critical. POWER is a mnemonic strategy to encourage students to proceed through the writing task in small steps. This strategy gives students the power to succeed when writing by encouraging them to use an organized, systematic process.[1]

In mnemonic strategies such as POWER, each letter stands for a single step your child needs to perform. When introducing the strategy, model how to follow the steps and then encourage her to do it herself. Be sure your child understands each step before moving on to the next. After all of the steps, show your child how they come together to create the full strategy and explain how each letter in the mnemonic serves as a memory hint or hook to trigger each step.

Power: P Is Plan This stage includes preparation activities and the development of some background experience, with the goal of establishing enthusiasm for the topic. It also involves discussing the basic format and type of writing required by the task, followed by determining the steps needed to complete the task. In doing so, the student plans the focus of the task.

Power: O Is Organize   The goal of this stage is to identify and describe the parts of the task. Visual organizers such as a story web (you can print one out at www.knowledgeessentials.com) and color-coding can help your child better manage all of the pieces of information.

Younger students may focus on three primary parts: beginning, middle, and end. Older students may add other relevant components such as characters, setting, problem, solution, and theme.

Some basic criteria to consider when helping your child organize are to

- Begin with information or tasks that are more concrete and gradually increase the ones that are abstract.
- Begin by including fewer components and progressively add more.
- Begin with a smaller task or chunk and progressively increase the size of the pieces.

Power: W Is Write   Students write their paragraph or paper, elaborating the ideas developed in the stage above. It is important to include both adult feedback and self-feedback at this stage. Self-feedback is described below.

Power: E Is Edit   In the editing stage, have your child focus on a single component at a time. She will proofread the paper multiple times, each time with a different focus. This step is often the most difficult for students with learning challenges because they tend to "read" what they intended rather than what they actually wrote. A great deal of modeling, scaffolding (helping much more at the beginning, decreasing your help as you progress), and direct instruction is necessary to help your child develop the appropriate editing skills and to encourage reading through the paper more than once.

The use of a speaking component provides multisensory input and helps decrease your child's confusion when editing her own work. It also helps prevent her from "reading" what she intended to write instead of reading what she actually put on the page.

Power: R Is Revise   Many students attempt to avoid the revision stage. However, it is critical that they learn this task as a valuable component of written expression. Again, scaffolding, modeling, and direct instruction are very useful in helping them understand how to enhance their writing. Using a self-feedback form to record the number of changes she makes provides a concrete record of her progress in revising and enhancing her written products. Of course, changes need to be appropriate and add to the quality of the paper. You can find a self-feedback form at www.knowledgeessentials.com.

Math Skills

Math is just getting harder and harder with every passing year, and your child may be really frustrated. Math calculations depend on math rules and procedures. Calculations require logical thinking, and the rules and procedures require a good base of working memory, one or both of which may be problematic for your child. To help your child work through some of the problems, here are some helpful suggestions.

Math Skills Activities

Math Calculations

Students who experience difficulties with math calculations have problems with some or most of the following skills:

- Solving multidigit calculations that require "borrowing" (subtraction) and "carrying" (addition). You can't "borrow" or "carry" numbers without writing on your math problem. Is your child making the changes on the page? Practice this together and with manipulatives or by drawing.

- Misaligning numbers when copying problems from a chalkboard or textbook. Setting up a math problem is hard. You line the numbers up from the right-hand side, and when you read letters you start at the left-hand side. It can be very confusing. Try placing a small piece of tape on the right-hand side of your child's desk to help him remember to line the numbers up from the right. Also try using graph paper when writing math problems; it's hard to misalign the numbers when you have columns and rows to help you stay on track!

- Ignoring decimal points that appear in math problems. You can't have dollars without cents, and you wouldn't know what cents are without a decimal point. If your child is blocking decimals, start working with money. Adding and subtracting prices with dollars and change is the fastest way to reinforce decimals.

Math Rules and Procedures

Students with a math disability can also demonstrate a developmental delay with learning the rules and procedures for solving calculations or word problems. An example of a *math rule* includes "any number $\times 0 = 0$." A *procedure* includes the steps for solving arithmetic problems such as addition, subtraction, multiplication, and division. A delay means that the child may learn the rules and procedures at a slower rate than his peer group and will need assistance in mastering those rules and procedures. Help your child make a chart of the math rules he forgets. Let him use the chart to complete homework assignments.

"Please excuse my dear Aunt Sally" is a mnemonic phrase for helping your child remember the order of operations (math procedures).

Please—parentheses—work all parts of the problem that is in parentheses

Excuse—exponents—solve the exponents

My—multiplication—multiply

Dear—division—divide

Aunt—addition—add

Sally—subtraction—subtract

Make and use rule books. Ask your child to keep a notebook in which he writes math rules in his own words. Encourage your child to use these rule books during classroom or homework assignments by looking up the rule in the book and talking about it. A rule book could have a math vocabulary section and a strategy section for recording "tricks" that help with the operations and the steps involved in solving various calculations.

Eventually, your child can expand the rule book to include math properties (rules) such as:

THE COMMUTATIVE PROPERTY (FOR EXAMPLE, $3 + 4 = 7$ and $4 + 3 = 7$)

Math Language

Some children have trouble understanding the meaning of the language or vocabulary of mathematics (for example, greater than, less than, equals, equation). Unfortunately, unlike reading, the meaning of a math word or symbol cannot be inferred from the context. Your child has to know what each word or symbol means in order to understand the math problem and complete it correctly.

MATH SYMBOLS TO KNOW: $+, -, \times, *, \div, \neq, \geq, \geq, \infty, \langle, =, /, \rangle, \%, \Sigma$

The easiest way to learn what math symbols mean is to make some flash cards. Make one set of flash cards that have the math word on them and make another set of flash cards with the corresponding symbol. Try these activities:

1. You say the word and your child holds up the card with the symbol on it. Switch roles.

2. Play a memory game where a complete pair is comprised of the card with the math word on it and the card with the matching math symbol on it.

3. Use a large sheet of paper to write a math problem with no symbols. Ask your child to choose a symbol to place between (or around or beside) the numbers and then compute the problem.

Assessment

You know all about assessment. You have spent years in IEP meetings and listening to expert evaluations of your child. You have observed your child so much that you are thinking about building an observation deck outside of her room. Things change when you get to middle school, so it may be time for a refresher. Let's start with some selected daily assessments (Table 10.2).

Your child will also have annual assessments at school, and those results will be discussed and applied at your child's IEP meeting. You can really help the process by saving things throughout the school year that, when looked at as a whole, give extraordinary insight to your child and a context to the test scores. Some things you may want to save and analyze as a whole are the following:

- Writing samples
- Reading log (dated list of books your child has read)
- Vocabulary journal (try generating from spelling word lists)
- Examples of math assignments
- Artwork
- Letters to friends and family
- Photographs of your child alone and with friends and family (in order to gauge body language when your child is alone versus in a group)
- Child's journal
- Weekly calendars
- Unit and lesson tests from that school year

Table 10.2. Daily Assessments

Type of Assessment	What you might see	What you will want to do	What you should consider doing instead
Behavior	Disorganized and scatterbrained.	Organize every aspect of your child's life for him.	Giving your child tools such as daily assignment sheets and a big calendar. Ask to see what your child has filled in on the sheets and calendar daily.
Social interaction	Very babyish or very adult behaviors, both of which are inappropriately extreme.	Ground your child from anything related to the extreme behavior.	Help your child identify the way other kids in his grade interact and role-play a few situations so that he will feel prepared to handle the social interactions.
Educational performance	Sharp decline in subject-area skills previously mastered.	Be overtly frustrated with your child.	Check your child's organization. She may be missing work because of her new middle school environment. Implement a daily assignment sheet and get supplies color-coded and organized.
Classroom attitudes	Doesn't care about school.	Make him stay at school longer, until he likes it.	Talk to your child to see why he is disinterested in his classes. Perhaps the IEP placement is too high or too low to meet his needs.

- Standardized test scores
- Teacher communication

Note

1. Richards, Regina G. (2001). *L*˙*E*˙*A*˙*R*˙*N: Playful Strategies for All Students,* Second Edition. Riverside, CA: RET Center Press, pp. 74–75.

High School

11

Moving from middle school to high school is a milestone to be celebrated by parents and teenagers. If your teenager has a disability, this can also be a time of anxiety and uncertainty. High school is a time when the curriculum becomes more rigorous; academic demands require more independence, organization, and responsibility; and post–high-school decisions must be made. As a parent and a student, the thought of high-school expectations can be overwhelming. In this chapter, you and your teenager will find information to prepare you both for a smooth educational transition into the high-school years.

Students with learning disabilities regularly use compensation strategies to help them with their academic work. This section focuses on the various strategies you can use with your child to help develop and manage his academic, social, and emotional skills, and eventually learn to regulate these on his own.

Compensation Strategies

By the time your child is in high school, you may be less able to help with subject-area content (depth of materials and high-school aptitude). Your child is now used to having a learning disability, and it is time to focus on strategies that will help your child overcome some of the difficulties associated with it. For example, your child may find that it is difficult to listen to the teacher and take notes at the same time, because taking notes requires so much effort due to reading, writing, and spelling difficulties. These students often photocopy someone else's notes and compare them with their own to determine whether they missed anything important during class. Additionally, computers, tape recorders, or books on tape can assist your child with course content.

Students with learning disabilities memorize information less successfully than other students. As such, other strategies become more important such as using flash cards, reviewing notes, planning time, asking peers for help, and reviewing text. All of these suggestions help develop the most important strategy of all: good work habits. Outlining the course content and using note cards are great strategies as well.

The next step is to empower your child by frankly discussing the nature of his disability. You should help your child understand

- The nature of his learning disability
- Her own profile of strengths and weaknesses
- The connection between his learning disability and academic performance

This understanding will give your child the knowledge he needs to be able to self-evaluate, manage time and work load, organize learning materials, keep records and monitor progress, create a proper study environment, rehearse and retain materials in routine and creative ways, review records and cluster materials, and find and use a support network. As you know by now, your child may have this knowledge but may not be able to implement it well. Gauge how much your child will be able to do on his own so that you can supplement his efforts if you need to.

Self-Regulation and Compensation Strategies

You can help your child begin developing a repertoire of personalized compensation strategies by doing such things as:

- Developing universal study skills
- Developing a personalized set of compensation strategies to promote academic success
- Steering clear of traditional remediation resource rooms because they tend to increase dependence rather than foster independence
- Promoting strategic learning and problem solving, and
- Exploring the benefits of assistive technology.

Creating a sense of self-determination within your child can be accomplished by:

- Helping your child develop self-advocacy skills
- Helping your child to set goals and then implement the plan to achieve them
- Teaching your child assertive communication, and
- Encouraging the student to reach for postsecondary education, whether it is a trade school or college.

Your child can develop greater independence by

- Taking a summer job to establish a work ethic
- Helping her understand the assessments that the school completes each year
- Asking your child to participate in IEP meetings, and
- Becoming aware of accommodations available for taking standardized tests.

Academic skills and strategies are important, but no less important than helping your child identify her own talents and social skills. It is high school after all!

Development and Enrichment Strategies

You can help your child enrich her academic life and recognize her own personal interests by encouraging her to

- Participate in extracurricular activities to broaden her horizons

- Participate in summer mentorship programs

- Become involved in extracurricular clubs, team sports, and speech or drama activities

- Evaluate her career interests through extracurricular activities, hobbies, and work experiences

- Explore interest and career inventories available through a high-school guidance counselor or bookstore, or you can find links to resources at www.knowledgeessentials.com.

- Participate in an enrichment program based on the student's strengths and interests

Social-Emotional Strategies

It's important to recognize and reinforce your child's social and emotional health and welfare. Help your child by

- Providing emotional support and encouragement if he is experiencing negative interactions with teachers or peers

- Stressing the importance of education and raising your child's aspirations

- Seeking support outside of school

- Offering help with schoolwork if needed

- Staying involved in your child's activities
- Nurturing your child's talents and interests
- Fostering your child's self-concept and self-esteem

Time-Management Skills

The academic demands of postsecondary education are far greater than those of most high schools. Students will be required to use note-taking, study, test-taking, and time-management skills that may not have been necessary in high school. It is important that students develop these skills before they begin classes at a postsecondary institution, and high school is a key time to focus on this area.

Day planner. We started using one in the middle-school chapter, and with any luck your child will still be using a day planner after she retires. It is the most practical way to organize her day.

Desk calendar. Whether it is a desk calendar or a desktop calendar (on his computer), your child should keep a visual reminder of how busy the days of the month are.

Assignment sheets. They were great in middle school and are still helpful in high school. The only difference here is that your child shouldn't need her teacher to sign off on them daily anymore. Try once a week, if at all.

School, home, and work schedule. Your child has distinct components of the day that should be treated with equal organizational importance. Remember, in just a few short years your child will need to manage his entire day on his own, so start working on that now.

Color-coding. Color-coding is easy, practical, and pretty. Color-code different subjects or schoolwork versus extracurricular work, and so on. Who wouldn't want things color-coded?

Life Skills

Many students with disabilities will not continue their educational career past high school. As such, you need to focus in depth on helping your child attain the skills necessary to live on his own. We are not talking about getting up and getting dressed each day, although that may be something you need to work on; we are talking about teaching your child to take care of herself to the point that she can live on her own. Examples of life skills include

Employment: finding and applying for jobs, interviews, and going to work everyday

Financial management: managing a bank account and paying bills

Housing: finding an apartment or a house and learning how to maintain a home

Shopping: buying groceries, toiletries, and other basic necessities on a regular basis

Healthcare: making appointments and going to the doctor on a regular basis, shopping for over-the-counter medicines and filling prescriptions, and managing other aspects of his healthcare

Relationships: dating, having and maintaining a relationship, and being sexually active

You and your child may miss the structure of school when graduation occurs, but it isn't as hard if you start planning for it early, which is what we will be doing in Chapter Twelve!

Exiting Special Services   12

In every circumstance the transition from high school to the real world is exciting and scary. For students with disabilities the transition is just as exciting, but it takes a lot of planning and coordination to give your child the support to make her entrée into the real world a successful experience. Even though a disabled student's transition is more involved, just like every part of his education, there is no magic formula that fits all students. Transitioning from high school is unique for every person and should capitalize on a person's strengths, weaknesses, interests, talents, and goals for the future.

Transitioning from High School to the Real World

Transition services are a plan or blueprint containing long-term goals and a coordinated set of activities and services designed to promote a successful transition from high school to postsecondary education or employment and independent living. Transition services will help you and your teen prepare for life after high school. Is your teen interested in going to college? Does he want to learn a specific skill or trade to gain employment? Does she need instruction in everyday life skills such as personal care, financial management, or community participation? By asking and answering these questions, you and your teen are creating a vision or goal for his future. This vision must be centered on your teen and grounded in his interests, strengths, and preferences. By identifying and understanding these factors, your teen—with the help of the IEP team—can develop a results-oriented plan that provides the necessary academic and functional skills to promote his maximum adult independence.

IDEA clearly states that transition planning must start by the time your child is sixteen. IEP teams must include transition planning in the first IEP that will be in effect when your teen turns age sixteen. Although this is the legal requirement, transition planning can begin earlier if deemed appropriate by the IEP team.

By age sixteen the IEP must address your teen's post-school vision, preferences, and interests. Think of it as a "vision statement." This vision statement focuses on your teen's post-school vision, preferences, and interests. Where does your child want to live, learn, and work? If your child will be living in assisted living, how will she be involved in the community? This vision statement is based on age-appropriate assessments related to training, education, employment, and independent-living skills, if appropriate. Assessments may include interest inventories, personal interviews, and other tools that can help acquire information about your teen's preferences. You should also provide information that will assist in determining your teen's preferences and interests.

This information, along with your teen's post-school vision, helps design measurable goals that are results-oriented and child-centered. The plan includes the type of instruction and educational experiences (a course of study) your teen will need to meet his postsecondary vision. Your teen's secondary courses will be selected and will reflect the core academic subjects and elective classes that will better prepare him for his post-school plan. Your teen will also be referred to your state's vocational rehabilitation counselor for possible vocational rehabilitation assessments and evaluations. Ask your IEP team or check your state's department of education about your state's guidelines. The next phase of transition moves from planning a vision, creating measurable goals, and identifying course work into developing a broad long-term goal, identifying the service areas needed, and coordinating services and activities.

Once a vision statement is formed, the IEP team must create a transition statement. A transition statement addresses the services needed to assist your teen in reaching his vision and goals. On the forms you fill out, this is commonly called a *Statement of Intended Results*. A transition statement (long-range goal) must be included in the IEP, based on your child's preference. It is important to consider your child's needs and desires and shift the focus of the IEP to what he wants in adult life. This statement should describe the intended result your teen is trying to achieve to meet his post-school vision and goals. This statement is supported by indicating the planning areas or transition-service areas that need to be addressed. There are five areas commonly addressed:

1. *Instruction.* The free and appropriate education in the least restrictive environment that your child is entitled to receive.

2. *Community experience.* Services that are provided outside of the school building, in community settings by schools or other agencies.

3. *Development of employment and other post-school living objectives.* Services that lead to a job or career, and important adult activities. These services are provided by schools and other organizations.

4. *Acquisition of daily living skills.* Services that teach your child the activities that adults do every day. Your child can obtain some of these skills in school by taking classes such as home economics or driver's education. Schools and other agencies provide these services.

5. *Functional vocational evaluation.* An assessment that provides information about job or career interests, aptitudes, and skills. Schools and other agencies provide these kinds of services.

After developing the transition statement and deciding the service area(s) that need to be addressed, the team develops a *coordinated set of activities.* A coordinated set of activities can simply be described as a set of strategies that promote transition into the adult world. The activities needed to promote a smooth transition for your teen can include:

- Specific curriculum participation, for example, elective keyboarding classes for students interested in data entry
- Vocational training such as cosmetology, food service, and automotive technician training
- Integrated employment such as sheltered workshops or job coaches
- Independent living skills such as driver's education, learning to use public transportation, or self-help activities, and
- Preparation for postsecondary education, such as designing a specific course plan to meet college entrance requirements, college application practice, and financial-aid meetings.

These activities are the building blocks for your teen's movement from a school to a post-school life.

After deciding the coordinated set of activities, the IEP team will identify who has the primary responsibility for each activity and specify the dates when each activity will begin and end. This information is commonly referred to as *linkages and responsible party(ies)* in the IEP. Knowing who will be involved in making these activities happen is an integral component of transition planning. It doesn't serve your teen well to have great plans and activities with no one accountable for following through. In addition to the IEP team (which must include the student) and school-based staff, responsible parties may include representatives from many community areas. Depending on your teen's goals, this could include higher-education counselors, officials from vocational and technology facilities, military representatives, state vocational rehabilitation counselors, or community-based employment representatives. Remember that planning for student needs with agencies takes a coordinated effort that is no easy undertaking. It is important to contact these agencies as soon as possible. This will allow sufficient scheduling time for their representatives to be able to attend the IEP meetings. These agents may be responsible for the delivery of some services provided to your teen. If these agencies fail to provide the agreed-upon transition services, it is the school district's responsibility to find an alternative way to meet your teen's transition goals. The IEP team must reconvene, identify alternate strategies, and amend the IEP.

This is an important place to emphasize your role in advocating for your teen. Actively include your family in the planning and decision making. Genuine parent and student participation is the critical element for successful transition into the adult world. The more involved you are in transition planning, the more effectively you can monitor your teen's progress and supervise the implementation of coordinated activities and services provided by outside agencies. Your active involvement ensures that the building blocks to your teen's future are actually building an edifice and not standing still. The following checklist will help you navigate through transition planning.

Checklist

Early Transition Planning (for Students in Middle School)

- ☐ Have your child's strengths and interests been adequately identified? If not, what assessments are needed?

- ☐ Can your child's strengths and interests generate ideas for realistic goals or directions for the future?

- ☐ Can your child expect to graduate with a regular high-school diploma?

- ☐ What would your child need to learn or be able to do in order to meet his or her goals?

☐ Does your child's course of study contribute to meeting these goals?

☐ Is self-advocacy training included in your child's program?

☐ If needed, are functional skills (for example, working with or managing money, shopping, using public transportation, and knowing how to be safe at home and in the community) included in your child's program?

☐ Are extracurricular activities relevant to your child's interests available?

Late Transition Planning (for Students in the Last Two Years of High School)

All of the above questions are still relevant, and additional ones need to be addressed:

☐ Can your child explain the specific nature of his or her disability? Does your child know when it is appropriate to disclose and discuss this disability and explain the accommodations it requires?

☐ Does your child know his or her legal rights?

☐ Have you and your child established working relationships with professionals from community-service agencies who will be providing services after your child leaves high school?

☐ Are there natural supports available in your community (friends, clubs, religious organizations, and so on) to meet your child's needs and interests?

☐ If your child has been using assistive technology or software, what arrangements have been made to ensure that these will be available to him or her after high school?

☐ If your child has reached your state's age of majority, has he or she received a notice of the rights that transfer?

An outline of a Transition Service Plan:

I. Address the student's post-school vision. (Vision statement) Live, work, learn? College, technical school, business school?

II. Information and activities used to develop a plan based on student preferences and interests. (Interest inventory, interview)

III. Create measurable, results-oriented goals to be listed in the IEP.

IV. Address the course of study. (Core classes and electives)

V. Referral to the vocational rehabilitation counselor.

VI. Statement of intended result. (Long-term goal)

VII. Transition services needed to support V. (Five common areas)

VIII. Coordinated activities (Building blocks)

IX. Linkages and responsible parties

Choosing Colleges for Students with Disabilities

The number of high-school students with disabilities planning to continue their education in postsecondary schools is increasing every year. Whether your teen plans to attend vocational and career schools or a two- or four-year college or university, you and your teen need to be informed about rights and responsibilities and how postsecondary education is different from the public-school model that you are both familiar with. The postsecondary school shifts the focus of education from a "Free Appropriate Public Education" as described in IDEA to a focus of "appropriate academic adjustment" to ensure nondiscrimination against an otherwise qualified person with a disability, as defined in Section 504 of the Rehabilitation Act of 1973 and Title II of the Americans with Disabilities Act of 1990 (ADA). Postsecondary schools do not operate under IDEA, but under Section 504 and the ADA.

Therefore, the services they are required to provide are different. We will briefly describe some of the differences pertaining to Section 504 and ADA, but it is recommended that you research and know your rights and responsibilities described in these laws.

Admission. A postsecondary school cannot deny admission because of a disability. However, disability or not, everyone must meet the school's essential requirements for admission. This is an important fact to know because it should be a consideration when planning a post-school vision, goals, and coordinated activities in the IEP during your child's high-school years. If your child wants to attend a community college to earn an associate's degree, you must plan for the college's entrance requirements. What math course or foreign-language qualifications apply? Know these facts early on and plan for them.

Academic adjustments. A postsecondary school does not need to know about your disability unless you want the school to provide academic adjustments or provide accessible facilities. An academic adjustment is an accommodation to academic requirements or auxiliary aides that are necessary to ensure an equal opportunity to education. This is leveling the playing field for a student with a disability. Some examples of adjustments may include reducing the course load to nine hours instead of fifteen, providing note takers, providing recording devices to record lectures, early or priority registration, substituting courses, sign-language interpreters, adaptive software or hardware, or extended time for test taking. Academic adjustments do not lower expectations or alter the course requirements. An example of a disabled student who needs extended testing time due to slower processing would apply here. The school may be required to provide extended time limits in order for the student to process written information but is not required to change the fundamental content of the test. The school is not required to lower or waive essential requirements such as completing all course requirements and being tested on course content.

Colleges are not required to make all the accommodations that public schools are required to provide, especially if they were to result in an undue financial or administrative burden. They do not have to provide students with aids or services that are of a personal nature such as tutors, personal assistants, or readers for personal use. If your child needs these services, the college should be able to refer you to quality resources. Of course, each situation or individual circumstance is unique, so you must have an idea of the academic adjustments you are seeking and find out how your needs can be met within the framework of Section 504 and ADA.

Usually, postsecondary schools require that you or your child follow a procedure to request academic adjustments. It is important to contact your child's chosen school and find out their procedures during your child's senior year of high school, or you may miss important deadlines for application or documentation submission. If you request academic adjustments, you will probably be required to provide documentation about your child's current disability and need for adjustments.

How Can You Help Your Child Be Successful in College?

The biggest key to success for students in college who have learning disabilities include things such as self-evaluation, organizing material, transforming material (for example, using flash cards), goal setting and planning, seeking information, keeping records and monitoring, structuring the environment, and using self-rewards along with rehearsing and memorizing.

There are many compensation strategies for students with disabilities. Some of them are as follows:

Environmental and social support and study skills: learning how to get around campus; learning where to go for services and when it is appropriate to ask for assistance; asking professors for lecture notes; requesting help from teaching assistants; using office hours to clarify assignments; asking others which professors are more understanding and accommodating of learning disabilities

Study strategies: learning library skills; developing personalized strategies for taking exams; learning ways to manage course materials (for example, using color-coded binders)

Cognitive and memory strategies: chunking material and time; monitoring assignments; using mnemonics; rehearsing; using flash cards

Time-management strategies: using weekly and monthly organizers

Note taking and written expression strategies: note taking; condensing notes; clustering material for exams; using graphical organizers in notes with the help of computer programs; highlighting in notes; color-coding notes and flash cards

Performance strategies for written expression, reading, comprehension, and mathematical processing: using concept maps to organize material and see connections among concepts; using the SQ3R method (survey, question, read, recite, review); doing repeated readings if necessary; writing one's own essays to ensure a deep understanding of the material; teaching the material to peers

Seeking instructors who use instructional adaptations (for example, alternative responding modes and modified instructional materials)

Reading and comprehension: using speech synthesis programs, optical character recognition programs, and variable-speech tape recorders (depending on the nature and severity of the learning disability)

Written language: making use of word processing, word-prediction software, spell-checking, speech or voice-recognition software, and outlining and concept-mapping software

Mathematics: using talking calculators; doing word problems

Personal organization: using personal data managers (software or handheld units such as a PDA), free-form databases (for example, computerized post-it systems), electronic reference materials, and web-based access; taking tests on a laptop computer

As you know from your years of raising a child with learning disabilities, a great deal of your child's success depends on her personal motivation to succeed. Here are a few pointers:

- Learn to use strategies designed to maintain effort for achieving goals: environmental (for example, block out distractions), attention (focus attention), and emotion (improve physical or emotional readiness to learn).

- Recognize that personalized compensation strategies equal academic success and require personal adjustment.

- Become aware that self-awareness and compensation strategies help promote success not only in academic but also in professional settings.

- Explore interests in greater depth to help foster motivation.

Your child is growing up and he is responsible for his own success. Here are some things that you should encourage your child to do for himself:

- Disclose learning disabilities to access services and ensure access to accommodations.

- Discuss one's learning disabilities with the instructor during office hours.

- Discuss the nature of the course requirements during office hours.

- Research which instructors and professors make accommodations for courses.

- Make use of the course materials posted by the instructor online.

- Take note that distance-learning courses may be particularly difficult for students with learning disabilities.

- Request a note taker, if applicable.

- Request carbon note paper for someone else to take notes.

- Tape-record lectures, particularly if material is difficult; request transcription services.

- Use a laptop in class for taking notes.

- Request seating in front if the instructor assigns seating in a lecture hall.

- Make use of computer labs and ask qualified personnel for help, if needed, in terms of word processing, completion of class assignments, and accessing and using Internet resources.

- Utilize assistive technology to enhance learning in computer labs or the disability services office.

- Access books on tape and e-texts via the college's resources or the Recording for the Blind and Dyslexic office, if applicable.

- Utilize the full range of services offered by a comprehensive college learning-disabilities support program.

- Request a private dorm room to minimize distractions.

- Access the help of tutors via the college's resource pool.

Strategies for ensuring testing considerations:

- On approval of the college learning-disabilities support program, request testing accommodations in terms of extended time on tests; alternative testing locations; and alternative format, content, and mode of presentation (visual or auditory) of the test.

- Discuss an alternative way to demonstrate course mastery if applicable, such as doing a course project instead of the multiple-choice exam, or doing an oral presentation, and so forth.

- Be sure to consider the college's program requirements and review the college's policy to determine options for the following:

- Request reduced course load and course substitution(s), if applicable.
- Request priority registration.
- Explore accommodations in the area of financial aid.
- Request course substitution(s).
- Request accommodations in a field or clinical setting or an internship in advance.

College is the time in our lives when we need some pretty serious social and emotional strategies to make friends, successfully complete the curriculum, and figure out what we do best. These issues are just as important as the academic issues, and your child needs your help to successfully consider them all and plan for them.

Social and emotional strategies that can be affected by parental actions are to

- Avoid unhealthy pressure for exclusivity of the top grades
- Encourage your student to stay resilient and persistent in the face of difficulties
- Nurture the student's talents and interests
- Foster the student's self-concept and self-esteem
- Help the student associate the benefits of using compensation strategies with academic success and personal adjustment
- Reframe a learning disability in a positive sense, and
- Foster the development of the student's personal characteristics (determination, resilience, integrity, work ethic, and social skills)

You and your child should be working to develop the talent that represents your child's strengths. You and your child should

- Continue exploring and nurturing talents and abilities

- Work with a mentor on a project in an area of interest
- Select a major considering one's personal profile of strengths and weaknesses
- Explore and nurture talents in other places, and
- Create a personal plan for academic success (your own IEP).

Documentation

Different schools require different levels of documentation. Some require more than others. Although IEP's and Section 504 plans can offer valuable information regarding what may have been effective in high school, they are not sufficient documentation. What was effective in high school may not be effective at the postsecondary school because the demands and setting are quite different. Be prepared to provide documentation that includes the following criteria stated in Section 504 of the Rehabilitation Act:

1. Documentation prepared by a professional psychologist, medical doctor, or other qualified diagnostician
2. Diagnosis of your child's current disability
3. Date of the diagnosis and how the diagnosis was concluded (educational testing or medical evaluation or both)
4. How your child's disability affects major life activities (learning, walking, speaking, breathing, working, performing manual tasks, or caring for oneself)
5. How the disability affects your child's educational performance

A word of caution, especially to learning-disabled students! Sometimes difficulty arises when the educational evaluations, such as the battery of tests that helped diagnose a student's learning disability, are not current. Many students are diagnosed with a learning disability in elementary or middle school and never formally reevaluated by a diagnostician. This doesn't mean that your school district was not in compliance; it means that information regarding a student's disability at the time of a student's reevaluation was sufficient to continue eligibility for special-education services.

Know the date of your child's last formal educational evaluation; if it is more than three years old, you will probably need a current evaluation. Know this in advance and plan for it. We will discuss this in more detail further in the chapter. Current information will help you and the school decide what appropriate academic adjustments will accommodate your child's disability and help ensure few if any delays in meeting your child's educational needs. This information may sound grim and scary and very different from the familiar model of secondary special education, but keep in mind that most postsecondary schools are very accommodating and will support your teen's pursuit of higher education.

Preparing for Postsecondary Education

Now that we have reviewed some of the basic differences in the laws that govern high school and postsecondary school, we can move on to the important aspects of being prepared for postsecondary education. Moving from high school to postsecondary can be an overwhelming time for students with disabilities and their families, but by understanding the differences, and preparing and planning for the new challenges, this transition can be managed.

Postsecondary education poses many challenges for students with disabilities, most significantly a responsibility challenge. Your teen will arrive at college or another postsecondary facility and be considered a responsible adult! Your teen is expected to be responsible for organization, time management, course requirements, and knowing how to learn on his own—yes, on his own! This is one of the major differences between high school and postsecondary school: managing academic tasks and advocating for accommodations shifts from the parent to solely the student. No phone calls will come from the teacher or special case manager to monitor your teen. Therefore, it is crucial for your teen's postsecondary success to prepare for this challenge during the high-school years by actively engaging in the planning and implementing of his IEP. While his IEP won't follow him to college, the knowledge he gains about himself and his disability will. This information will help prepare him to be an advocate for what he can do and what he needs help with. To help you and your teen manage this transition, a basic plan or road map can be described as Prepare, Plan, Choose.

Prepare

1. Teach self-advocacy and self-determination skills. Your teen should understand his disability. This includes knowing how the disability affects learning. Knowing his areas of strengths and weakness can help identify things that are challenging. This can lead to an increased ability to articulate his needs. Good communication skills and knowledge of his disability are critical.

2. Teach your teen to use and seek accommodations in challenging areas such as note taking or reading text. Seek technology that can help compensate for his disability such as laptops with special software.

3. Identify strategies that are effective for your teen relating to time management, study skills, and organization. There are many great resources that provide specific detailed strategies based on your teen's unique needs.

4. Help your teen to understand the fundamental differences between high school and postsecondary school. Discuss changes in the academic environment. For example, it is less physically structured with no bells and no assigned seating. The majority of his work will be completed outside of class, and he will have less contact with his instructor.

Plan

1. Plan for postsecondary education during the high-school years by using the transition-services planning component of your teen's IEP. Ask about and plan for activities that will prepare your teen. Work closely with the school staff to implement these activities.

2. Plan to contact the admissions office of several postsecondary schools. Ask for the following information regarding:

   a. Admission process and procedures for students with disabilities

   b. Required documentation for the disability

   c. Services or organizations that the school offers for students with disabilities.

3. Plan to have current educational or medical testing completed. This may mean discussing your teen's plans with your doctor in order to obtain the medical documentation for the disability. As mentioned previously, if your teen has a learning disability it is important to discuss obtaining new educational testing with the IEP team before your teen graduates. It is usually a good idea to initiate new testing during the student's junior year. Most schools are accommodating, but by law do not have to provide new testing. You may have to seek a private evaluation that you pay for.

4. Plan to discuss vocational rehabilitation guidelines with the IEP team. IDEA states that disabled students must be referred to the state's vocational rehabilitation counselor no later than their sixteenth birthday. If your teen meets your state's vocational rehabilitation guidelines, he may be eligible for financial assistance and other supports.

5. Plan to contact the Social Security Administration to see whether your teen meets the guidelines for a disability and may be eligible for support.

6. Plan to request testing accommodations for college entrance exams such as the ACT or SAT.

7. Plan to disclose your disability to postsecondary schools if you need support. It is best to disclose this early on rather than wait until it is too late.

Choose

1. Choose by comparing what is offered at postsecondary schools such as the courses of study or the services offered to disabled students.

2. Choose by comparing postsecondary school requirements. Entry and completion requirements vary from school to school.

3. Choose by visiting postsecondary schools and speaking with faculty, advisors, or other students with similar disabilities. This can often reveal the real commitment level that schools have to disabled students.

4. Choose by asking questions generated by you and your teen that are relevant to your situation. A few examples might be:

  a. Who provides tutorial support? Interns, graduate students, peer tutors?

  b. What are the typical accommodations made for your child's particular disability?

  c. Where does the student go when he needs assistance?

Attending postsecondary school is an important and attainable goal for many students with disabilities. By preparing and planning for postsecondary education early, and choosing a facility that meets your teen's unique abilities and needs, you and your teen are increasing his opportunities to be successful in the adult world.

ACRONYMS

Acronym	What it stands for	Definition
A		
AAD	adaptive assistive devices	Devices that assist people with disabilities in better functioning at school, work, and life. Devices may include wheelchairs, artificial limbs, Braillers, low-vision devices, hearing aids, educational devices, and adapted toys.
AAT	advanced academic training	Special-education teachers often have specialized training in their field that goes beyond the normal teacher requirements. The training may focus on psychology, legal issues, special-needs development, and skills needed to work with and teach children with disabilities.
ABA	applied behavior analysis	This is the application of examining human behavior through the principles of science. ABA is used to improve social behaviors, including reading, social skills, living skills, and communication.
ABD	antisocial behavior disorders	This is generally characterized by a lack of socialization, discord with social values, disregard of the law and rights of others, and refusal to acknowledge guilt or responsibility for his or her actions. Typically, the characteristics of this behavior appear before the age of fifteen, but may not be diagnosed until much later.

(continued)

(continued)

Acronym	What it stands for	Definition
ABE	adult basic education	This is instruction in skills such as writing, reading, math, and other skills necessary to function in society. The instruction is usually given to people over the age of sixteen.
ACT	American College Testing	This is a test high-school students take to assess their educational development and their capacity to complete college-level work. ACT does serve students with disabilities by providing appropriate accommodations to meet the student's disability.
AD	attachment disorder	A serious problem with emotional attachments to others. This can be a child who is overly friendly with everyone, including strangers, or a child who is mistrustful of everyone. The disorder is associated with the failure in infancy or early childhood of the child to bond with the caretaker.
ADA	Americans with Disabilities Act; average daily attendance	Civil rights protection for individuals with disabilities; the cumulative attendance during a typical school year divided by the number of days the school is in session.
ADC	Aid to Dependent Children	A program that was established by the U.S. Congress under Title IV of the Social Security Act to give cash assistance to low-income families.
ADD	attention deficit disorder	A disability that affects a child's ability to concentrate and control behavior. The child often has trouble sustaining attention in connection with school, play, and normal life tasks.
ADHD	attention deficit with hyperactivity disorder	The presence of hyperactivity in attention deficit disorder.
ADL	activities of daily living	These are tasks of everyday life, like dressing, eating, bathing, etc.
ADR	alternative dispute resolution	This is a term used to describe a way of resolving an issue outside of court. This may include mediation, negotiation, or conciliation.
ADVOC-NET	adult vocational network	A network of vocational services for adults with special needs.

Acronym	What it stands for	Definition
AEA	acquired eleptiform aphasia (Landau-Kleffner syndrome)	A rare neurological disorder that causes the loss of the ability to understand speech and a deterioration of language skills. Most children also suffer from epileptic seizures.
AEP	alternative education placement	A program designed to offer an alternative to the traditional classroom setting. Primarily used for students who have had behavior problems.
AFDC	Aid to Families with Dependent Children	This program provides financial assistance to disadvantaged families. This is what was commonly known as welfare and was replaced in 1997 by TANF (Temporary Assistance for Needy Families).
AFS	adult and family services	Usually a program that provides assistance and social services to adults, children, and families.
AG	annual goal	Relates to the present level of performance of the child and sets the direction for future performance. It also provides a way to determine if goals are being met.
AHSD	adult high school diploma	A program that enables an adult to complete required courses to earn a high school diploma.
AI	auditorily impaired	Refers to serious hearing loss.
AIDS	Acquired Immune Deficiency Syndrome	AIDS is the final stage of the HIV.
ALO	alternative learning options	Alternative ways for students who do not fit into the traditional educational programs to continue in school. These can include alternative schools, special classes, telecommunication courses, and other programs.
ALS	advanced life support	Emergency medical care administered to sustain life.
AMD	alternative mobility device	Devices such as canes, adapted canes, or other mobility devices for children who are blind or severely visually impaired.
AP	advanced placement	A test used to measure skills and knowledge that may exceed the content of the standards of learning, allowing the student to earn advanced standing in college.

(continued)

(continued)

Acronym	What it stands for	Definition
APD	antisocial personality disorder; auditory processing disorder	Antisocial personality disorder: This is generally characterized by a lack of socialization, discord with social values, disregard of the law and rights of others, and refusal to acknowledge guilt or responsibility for his or her actions. Typically, the characteristics of this behavior appear before the age of fifteen, but may not be diagnosed until much later. Auditory processing disorder: A disorder that prevents one from recognizing subtle differences between sounds in words.
APE	adaptive physical education	This is physical education (PE) that is modified to address the needs of children who have disabilities that prevent them from performing in normal PE activities.
APPE	average per pupil expenditure	The amount of money expended for on each student, usually calculated from the school district's financial report.
ARD	admission, review, and dismissal (committee)	A committee including the student's parents and school personnel that will determine the student's eligibility to special education services. The committee will develop an Individualized Education Plan (IEP) for the student.
ARP	advisory review panel	This panel is responsible for advising the state superintendent of public schools in ways to accommodate and promote services for special needs children. This includes implementing IDEA.
ASC	advanced study center	Usually a center that focuses on research and further education of a particular study, such as special needs.
ASD	autism spectrum disorder	A severe impediment in the ability to relate to others, including thinking, speaking, and feeling.
ASDO	alternative service delivery options	The assurance that alternative placement is available as well as supplementary services to special-needs students.
ASL	American Sign Language	Visual-spatial language that is used by the hearing impaired.
AT	assistive technology	An item or device that may be customized or modified to assist people with disabilities. This includes text-to-speech screen readers, modified keyboards, voice recognition software, wheel chair ramps, and so on.
ATCP	alternative teacher certification program	A program designed to prepare teachers for expedited entry into teaching shortage areas, such as special education.

Acronym	What it stands for	Definition
AU	autistic	One who has autism.
AUT	autism	A neurodevelopmental disorder characterized by markedly abnormal social interaction, communication ability, patterns of interests, and patterns of behavior.
AVTI	area vocational technical institute	A school designed to teach vocational skill and techical trades.
AYP	annual yearly progress	A sum of the progress achieved throughout the year.
B		
BAC	behavior adjustment class	A class designed to isolate students from other students. The length and curriculum is designed by teachers and administrators.
BASIS	Basic Adult Skills Inventory System	A system used to determine literacy and comprehension skill levels.
BD	behaviorally disordered; behavior disorders; brain damaged	behaviorally disordered; behavior disorders: Behavior considered abnormal; violence, actions that are destructive and other socially unacceptable behavior. brain damaged: An injury to the brain that can be caused by various conditions and is often associated with abnormal behavior or function.
BEP	behavioral education plan	A plan generally designed to address special needs and at-risk students. The plan may require extra contact with a teacher, give more feedback, and involve parents to a greater degree.
BEST	basic education study team	Consultants or other qualified individuals who determine basic education needs and help school districts implement basic education plans.
BETAC	bilingual education technical assistance centers	Centers that provide assistance and education to individuals whose native language is not English.
BI	brain injury	An injury to the brain that may cause behavioral disorders.
BIA	Brain Injury Association; Bureau of Indian Affairs	Brain Injury Association—an association dedicated to providing resources and support to anyone suffering from brain damage and that person's family or caregiver; Bureau of Indian Affairs—government agency focused on Native Americans.

(continued)

(continued)

Acronym	What it stands for	Definition
BIL	bilingual	Able to speak more than one language.
BIP	behavior intervention plan	A plan resulting from background information about a student and his or her behavioral issues. This plan will include behavioral goals, intervention strategies, set reviews, and a method for evaluation of the plan.
BMP	behavior management plan	This plan is generally part of an IEP and addresses what may cause the behavior, what the behavior is, and what happens because of the behavior.
C		
CA	chronological age	The actual number of years a person has been alive. Sometimes used to measure behavior and intelligence.
CAI	computer-assisted instruction	A type of instruction that implements computers in some form of instruction.
CAM	certificate of advanced mastery	A certificate generally earned by students who have shown exceptional knowledge of skills in preparation for their future goals.
CAP	central auditory processing	The processing of information one hears.
CAPD	central auditory processing disorders; see also APD (auditory processing disorder)	The inability of the brain to correctly process what one is hearing.
CAT	committee on accessible transportation	A counsel designed to advise on the transportation needs and concerns of persons with disabilities.
CBA	curriculum-based assessment	A way to monitor a student's progress through the existing course content.
CBM	curriculum-based measurement	Used in making special-education decisions, CBM is a set of measurement procedures that gather data.
CC	cross-categorical	A program that allows special-need students with different areas of disability to be combined for delivery of services.
CD	communication development; conduct disorder	Conduct disorder: A disorder that causes children to behave in socially unacceptable ways and have difficulty following rules.

Acronym	What it stands for	Definition
CDA	child development associate	Someone who has trained in the basic principles of early childhood education.
CDRC	child development and rehabilitation center	A center designed to offer services and support to anyone with disabilities or special needs, while also offering resources for individuals, families, and communities.
CDS	child development specialist	A person trained to provide flexible services to families in order to help with parenting skills, developmental issues, and acquired disabilities.
CFLA	community and family living amendments	This bill was designed for individuals who have severe developmental or physical disabilities. It provides supplemental income and services to such individuals.
CFR	Code of Federal Regulations	The codification of the general and permanent rules published in the Federal Register by the executive departments and agencies of the Federal Government.
CHAP	child health assurance program	For those who qualify, this program provides Medicaid coverage to pregnant women and children below the age of six.
CHD	center on human development	Assists individuals with disabilities and special needs through research, clinical services, training, and other areas of need.
CHI	closed head injury	When the head suffers a blunt force by striking against an object.
CIL	center for independent living	A center that aids an individual with disabilities to live independently.
CIM	certificate of initial mastery	A certificate awarded to students who have met the initial perfomance standards on test and classroom work.
CLAS	culturally and linguistically appropriate services	An organization that promotes early intervention practices that are sensitive to children's and families' cultural and linguistic differences.
CLD	culturally and linguistically diverse	The difference in culture and language in various groups.
CMHP	community mental health program	A community organization designed to supply support and resources to individuals and families needing mental health services.
CNS	central nervous system	The body's spinal cord and brain.

(continued)

(continued)

Acronym	What it stands for	Definition
COTA	certified occupational therapist assistant	Someone who works under a registered occupation therapist to assist patients who may have psychosocial, physical, or cognitive impairments.
CP	cerebral palsy	A chronic disorder that impairs control of movement and posture. The disorder generally worsens over time.
CPPC	cooperative personnel planning council	A group who is generally made up of teachers, administrators, parents, and others who provides professional development and continuing education activities; technical assistance; coordinates with other interested groups. May also have budgetary responsibilities.
CPSE	committee on preschool special education	A committee focused on the needs, education, and early intervention of special-needs preschool students.
CSA	childhood sexual abuse	Sexual abuse at any time during childhood.
CSE	case study evaluation; committee on special education	Case study evaluation: A study that involves interviews with the child and child's parents, comprehensive report of the child's medical history, social development study, all health screenings, academic history achievement testing, and assessment of the child's learning process and environment. Committee on special education: Committee that assesses the needs and services for special education as well as sets and reviews guidelines.
CSEF	Center for Special Education Finance	Responsible for measuring special-education costs and expenditures; conducts policy analyses, collects and maintains financial information, and disseminates the information.
CSPD	comprehensive system of personnel development	Required by law, each state must have a system in place for special education that guarantees all education personnel are properly prepared to instruct as well as receive continuing education.
CSS	community support service	Assists individuals and families in finding community services and support.
CTT	community transition team	A group of individuals who help a special-needs student prepare for transition. This includes being informed about resources and adult services available in the community.

Acronym	What it stands for	Definition
D		
D&E	diagnosis and evaluation	A diagnosis is usually given by a health care provider after an exam and possibly further test. Evaluation is then given of the best form of treatment.
DAP	developmentally appropriate practices	These usually consist of implementing programs considered age appropriate for the individual child as well as consideration of social and cultural circumstances.
DARTS	day and residential treatment services	Day treatment is a service offered as an out patient service while residential treatment is for those who need care twenty-four hours a day.
DAS	developmental apraxia of speech	A speech disorder where a person has difficulty in saying what he or she wants to say correctly.
DB; DBL	deaf-blind	A person with little or no useful sight and hearing.
DCD	developmental coordination disorder	A disorder characterized by poor coordination.
D	deaf	Lacking the sense of hearing in whole or part.
DD	developmental disabilities; developmentally delayed	Developmental disability is having a severe disability consisting of mental or physical impairments, or in some cases, a combination of both. Developmentally delayed is when someone learns at a slower rate than others in his or her age group.
DDC	developmental disabilities council	A committee designed to implement plans for the inclusion of special-needs individuals in the community.
DDD	division of developmental disabilities	A division usually responsible for providing a variety of services to people with developmental disabilities. These may include residential services, family support, day programs, case management, and assistance in obtaining other services.
DHHAP	deaf and hard of hearing access program	Assists in adapting state and local programs to meet the communication needs of the hearing impaired.
DHR	Department of Human Resources	DHS is an agency responsible for protecting the health of citizens by providing various services.

(continued)

(continued)

Acronym	What it stands for	Definition
DI	direct instruction	An instructional procedure designed to provide students with specific instructions on an assignment or independent practice so that immediate feedback can be given.
DNR	do not resuscitate	A legal document signed by an individual or individual's caretaker requesting that no life-saving measures be taken.
DoDDS	US Dept. of Defense Dependent Schools	Schools operated by the Department of Defense. The schools can be found throughout the world and are for military civilians' dependent children. Most schools have special-education services.
DOE	Department of Education	This department is responsible for equal access to education as well as promoting educational excellence. There is a national department as well as one in each state.
DON	determination of need	This is a way to determine the socioeconomic need of individuals who need access to health care services.
DREDF	Disability Rights Education and Defense Fund	A legal center designed to protect and improve the civil rights of people with disabilities.
DRG	diagnostically related groups	Usually refers to certain classes of diagnoses and is related to the health care industry's billing practices.
DS	direction service	A service organization for people with disabilities and special needs that provides programs focusing on family support, information services, counseling and assessment, and other areas.
DSM	Diagnostic and Statistical Manual (for Mental Disorders)	Standard reference on the classification of mental disorders.
E		
EBD	emotional and behavioral disorders	A combination of behavioral and emotional disorders that cause an individual to be unable to control their emotions or control them enough to be socially acceptable.
EC	early childhood; exceptional child[ren]	The developmental period extending from the end of infancy to about five or six years of age; Children with exceptionalities, being either disabled and/or gifted.

Acronym	What it stands for	Definition
ECE	early childhood education	Education designed for children between the ages of two and six.
ECI	early childhood intervention	Programs that are designed to provide assistance to children with special needs, usually between the ages of infancy to five or six years.
ECSE	early childhood special education	Early childhood education focused on special-education students' needs and development.
ECT	early childhood team	A team responsible for designing programs that accommodate and improve the lives of children with special needs.
ED	emotionally disturbed; emotional disorders; U.S. Department of Education	Emotionally disturbed: a condition that prevents the building or maintaining of relationships; the individual may also exhibit inappropriate behavior or depression and develop fears or physical symptoms. Emotional disorders: a diagnosed disorder that affects the emotional stability of an individual. (U.S. Department of Education: National Department of Education.)
EDGAR	Education Department General Administrative Regulations	Federal regulations published by the U.S. Department of Education.
EEs	essential elements	Fundamental parts that make a plan, program, and so forth, work.
EEN	exceptional education needs	Refers to students who show a severe developmental delay.
EFA	experimental functional analysis	An experimental way of analyzing behavior problems.
EHA	Education for All Handicapped Children Act (since 1990, known as the Individuals with Disabilities Education Act [IDEA])	The Individuals with Disabilities Education Act.
EI	Early Intervention	This applies to school-age children or younger that have, or may be at risk of having, special needs. It applies to recognizing the problem and providing services and resources to the individual and family.
EI/ECSE	Early Intervention/early childhood special education	Childhood education focused on the special needs of the students.

(continued)

(continued)

Acronym	What it stands for	Definition
ELL	English language learner	An indivdual who may speak limited or no English and is currently learning the language.
EMDR	eye movement desensitization and reprocessing	An information processing therapy for certain types of personality disorders.
EMH	educable mentally handicapped	A student who has mild impairment in intelligence or social behavior and is capable of learning, usually two to three grade levels below.
EMR	educably mentally retarded	A student capable of learning to approximately sixth-grade level.
EMT	emergency medical treatment	Various types of emergency first aid or ICU.
EPSDT	early periodic screening diagnosis and treatment program	A program designed to recognize and help in early identification and treatment of medical and developmental issues in children.
EQ	exceptional quality	Exceeding the normal quality.
ERC	education resource center	A center dedicated to providing educational resources in certain areas, for example, special needs.
ERIC	Educational Resources Information Center	Sponsored by the Institute of Education Sciences (IES) of the U.S. Department of Education, ERIC produces and maintains a database of journal and nonjournal education literature.
ESA	education service agency	Usually a public agency that provides assistance with Early Intervention programs designed for students with disabilities.
ESC	education service center	An agency authorized by state statute and governed by participating school corporations to offer supplemental educational services.
ESD	education service district	A district or area that is served by the education service agency.
ESE	exceptional student education	This usually refers to services provided by a school for special-needs students as well as gifted students.
ESEA	Elementary and Secondary Education Act	This act allows money to be allocated to schools with a high amount of low-income children. This started several programs, such as Head Start.

Acronym	What it stands for	Definition
ESL	English as a second language	Someone whose native language is something other than English.
ESOL	English for speakers of other languages	A class or lessons geared for people who are learning English as a second language.
ETP	effective teaching practices	Practices designed to accommodate and help special-needs students.
ESY	extended school year	This term includes a range of options for providing programs in excess of the traditional school year.
EYS	extended year services (ECSE)	Services offered through extended school-year programs.
F		
FAIP	functional assessment and intervention program	A requirement by IDEA to be conducted before placement or suspension for students with disabilities.
FAPE	free appropriate public education	Under IDEA, all disabled children should receive a free and appropriate education.
FAST	functional academic skills test	A test composed of two sections that evaluates aspects of adaptive behavior involving the use of academically related acquired learning to the problems of issues related to daily living.
FBA	functional behavior assessment	A process used to address problem behavior in students. The purpose is to identify specific occurrences or nonoccurrences associated with specific behaviors.
FC	facilitated communication; foster care	An alternative means of expression for people who have extremely limited speech or no speech at all; a substitute form of care for children who are unable to live in their own homes.
FDAB	Fair Dismissal Appeals Board	A board, usually appointed by a state governor, of teachers and school administrators with jurisdiction to hear appeals from teachers and other school personnel regarding dismissals.
FERPA	Family Educational Rights to Privacy Act (aka the Buckley Amendment)	A federal law used to protect student records.

(continued)

(continued)

Acronym	What it stands for	Definition
FIPSA	Fund for the Improvement of Post-secondary Education	A fund to provide assistance for programs that are designed to improve access to and quality of postsecondary education.
FLSA	Fair Labor Standards Act	An act that provides for the minimum standards for workers, including wages, overtime, and child labor.
FMLA	Family Medical Leave Act	Requires employers to provide up to twelve weeks of unpaid leave and continued health coverage to employees when they are absent due to family matters.
FR	Federal Register	A daily publication for rules and notices of the federal government.
FSA	Family Support Act	Enforces child support laws.
FSHA	first source hiring agreement	Agreements designed to employ local residents first.
FSD	flexible service delivery model	A way of providing services to students who learn differently by using available school resources.
FTE	full-time equivalent	A measurement equivalent to one person working a full-time schedule for one year.
FY	fiscal year	Any yearly accounting period.
G		
GAPS	guardianship, advocacy, and protective services	Agencies created to address the issues of abuse, neglect, and lack of programming in institutions for learning-disabled people.
GSE	generic special education	A broad and general degree in special education.
GT	gifted and talented	Students who demonstrate an ability to learn at levels above their peers.
H		
HBCU	historically black colleges and universities	Any historically black college or university that was established prior to 1964 with the principal mission to educate black Americans.
HI	health impaired; hearing impaired	One who has health issues that affect daily life; one who has difficulty hearing or is deaf.

Acronym	What it stands for	Definition
HOH	hard of hearing	Little to no useful hearing abilities.
HOTS	higher-order thinking skills	A computer-based thinking program for students who are at risk. It emphasizes the basic thinking processes.
HS	Head Start; high school	A program designed to provide school readiness through comprehensive education, nutrition, health, and parent involvement to low-income families.
HSC	high school completion	Often a program offered to individuals who did not complete high school during the normal course of time.
I		
IASA	Improving America's Schools Act	An act that provided more help to disadvantaged students while holding schools accountable. It also included charter schools, drug-free programs, safety, technology, and bilingual programs.
IAES	interim alternative educational setting	A setting for a student who has been suspended from regular classroom activities.
ICC	interagency coordinating council	A council designed to advise and assist coagencies.
ICD	international code of diseases	The classification used to code and classify diseases.
ICDP	individual career development plans	A plan to recognize the interests and abilities of employees and strategically plan career goals and offer support for goal achievement.
ICF	intermediate care facility	A facility designed to provide care to individuals who do not need a hospital or more detailed care.
ICFMR	intermediate care facility for mental retardation	A facility that provides supervised care for mentally retarded individuals.
IDEA	Individuals with Disabilities Education Act	IDEA is the federal law designed to cover students with disabilities until they graduate from high school or until they reach age twenty-two. Special-needs and learning-disabled students are covered under the law, as well as others.
IDELR	Individuals with Disabilities Education Law Report (from LRP Pubs.)	A legal report, available through LRP.
IED	intermittent explosive disorder	A disorder that causes violent outbursts of rage.

(continued)

(continued)

Acronym	What it stands for	Definition
IEE	independent education evaluation	An evaluation conducted by an examiner who is not an employee of the school the child is attending.
IEP	individualized education program	A program that brings a team of special-education professionals as well as the parents or caretakers of the child to determine an education plan.
IEPC	individualized educational planning committee	Special-education professionals, parents, caretakers, and anyone else who is involved in the child's education.
IEU	intermediate educational unit	A unit designed to provide services to meet the diverse educational needs of students.
IFA	individualized functional assessment	An assessment that describes the challenging behaviors and provides such information as times, events, and situations that are related to them.
IFSP	Individualized Family Service Plan	A program that provides Early Intervention and information about necessary services a child will need.
IHE	institution of higher education	A university or college that provides an academic degree.
IHCP	individualized health care plan	Private insurance for an individual or family.
IHO	impartial hearing officer	Someone who has authority to participate in a hearing and does not have a personal or professional interest in it.
IHP	individualized habilitation program or plan	A plan or program designed to correspond with a person's capacities.
IHTP	individualized habilitation and treatment plan	A treatment plan based on a person's capacities to help him or her have a meaningful life.
ILC	independent living center	A center that provides services and advocacy for persons with all types of disabilities.
ILP	independent living plan	A plan that will provide services and support for the transition of a special-needs person living independently.
ILT	instructional leadership training	A program that trains professionals with skills and knowledge used to guide teachers, aides, or paraprofessionals in their efforts to improve a student's education.
IMC	instructional materials center	A center that supports education through various forms of instruction, including technology.

Acronym	What it stands for	Definition
IML	instructional materials laboratory	A center that may house computers and other technology devices.
IPE	individualized plan for employment	Using information gathered during assessment, this tool helps determine appropriate employment.
IPL	initial program load	Generally used as a term referring to the loading of a mainframe operating system into a computer's main memory.
IPP	individualized program plan	A plan designed to meet individual needs, usually for education, transitions, and independent living.
IQ	intelligence quotient	Indicates a person's mental abilities compared to others of approximately the same age.
ISP	individualized service plan	A plan for a person with developmental disabilities that details what he or she wants to achieve and ways to accomplish it.
ISS	in school suspension	When a student will remain on the school premises, but not in a typical classroom with other students.
ITH	intensive training home	A residence committed to providing comprehensive training to people with developmental disabilities.
ITIP	instructional theory into practice	Using a theory in teaching.
ITP	individualized transition plan (similar to IEP)	A plan designed to detail a person's transition into leaving school, living alone, and so on.
J		
JDRP	joint dissemination review panel	A panel designed to make recommendations about effective educational programs.
JOBS	job opportunities and basic skills	A program that teaches basic skills and provides various resources for finding employment.
JTPA	Job Training Partnership Act	An act created to improve the opportunities of certain individuals in obtaining employment.
JJAEP	juvenile justice alternative education	A program that takes at-risk students and works to rehabilitate them with the goal of getting them placed back in their original school districts.

(continued)

(continued)

Acronym	What it stands for	Definition
L		
LA	language arts	The study of reading, writing, and speaking.
LD	learning disabilities; learning disabled	A disability that causes a student to be intellectually behind his or her age group; having a learning disability.
LDA	Learning Disabilities Association	An organization designed to provide support and resources for parents, students, professionals, and individuals with learning disabilities.
LDP	language development program	A program designed to help a student develop proficiency in the English language.
LEA	local education agency	An agency that has resources and information on local education.
LEDS	law enforcement data system	A data system that shares data with both local and national agencies.
LEP	limited English proficient	A limited use of the English language.
LICC	local interagency coordinating council	A council designed to coordinate local agencies.
LIFE	living in functional environments	Teaching individuals with disabilities life skills that are age-appropriate and enhance the individual's ability to live functionally.
LoF	Letter of Finding issued by the Office for Civil Rights (OCR)	A letter confirming the finding, or lack thereof, of a civil-rights complaint.
LPTA	licensed physical therapy assistant	A trained and licensed assistant to a physical therapist.
LRE	least restrictive environment	An educational setting where special-needs children can receive a free appropriate public education that is designed to meet the child's educational needs without putting the student in a special educational environment.
LSSP	licensed specialist in school psychology	A school specialist who concentrates on psychology.
LTCF	long-term care facility	A facility designed to care for an individual for an extended period of time or possibly on a permanent basis.

Acronym	What it stands for	Definition
LTCT	long-term care and treatment	Treatment and care of someone in a long-term care facility.
M		
MA	mental age	A level of intellectual development based on the results of an IQ test.
MBD	minimal brain dysfunction	A condition characterized by learning disorders or behavior disorders.
MBO	management by objective	A structured method of setting goals.
MDC	multi-disciplinary conference	A conference encompassing several disciplines.
MDT	multidisciplinary team; manifest determination team	A group of professionals from diverse backgrounds who work together for a common purpose; a team that determines what causes behavior to manifest and how to address it.
M/ED	mental or emotional disturbance	A condition that includes the inability to learn, inability to build and maintain relationships, inappropriate types of behavior, and so on.
MESC	migrant education service center	A center focused on educational services provided to migrant children.
MFCU	medically fragile children's unit	A section of a hospital or care center dedicated to caring for physical health impairments.
MH	multiply handicapped	Individuals with more than one disability.
MHM	multihandicapped mainstream	Someone who has multiple handicaps but functions in the mainstream society.
MHMR	mental health mental retardation	The focus of mental health services and resources for individuals who are mentally retarded.
MI	multiple intelligences	A theory that proposes humans have several different types of intelligences.
MIS	management information systems	A system or network of communication channels used by an organization.
MMR	mild mental retardation	A lesser form of mental retardation.
MMS	mastery management system	A tool teachers use to track which skills your child has mastered.

(continued)

(continued)

Acronym	What it stands for	Definition
MR	mentally retarded or mental retardation	Mental impairment that prevents an individual from participating at the same level as others of the same age.
MR/DD	mentally retarded/developmentally disabled	Mental impairment that prevents an individual from participating at the same level as others of the same age.
MR/MED	mentally retarded and mentally or emotionally disturbed (sometimes referred to as dual diagnosis)	Having behavioral issues along with mental impairment.
MSDD	multisystem developmental disorder	Individuals who are not autistic, but have communication, social, and sensory processing problems.
MSRTS	migrant student record transfer system	A nationwide information network that maintains and transfers education information from school to school for migrant children.
MST	multisystemic therapy	A family-based treatment that addresses known determinants of antisocial behavior, such as environment and other factors.
N		
NCES	National Center for Education Statistics	A center that collects, analyzes, and makes available data related to education.
NCLB; NCLBA	No Child Left Behind Act	A law that basically sets new standards of learning for children and requires all states to comply to these standards, as well as the other requirements of the act.
NDT	neurodevelopmental treatment	An advanced therapeutic approach to treating individuals who, because of neurological issues, have difficulty controlling movements.
NEA	National Education Association	U.S. labor union committed to advancing the cause of public education.
NICU	neonatal intensive care unit	A unit where premature infants and other critically ill infants are cared for.
NSBA	National School Boards Association	A nationwide organization representing public school governance.

Acronym	What it stands for	Definition
O		
O&M	orientation and mobility	Refers to blind, deaf, or blind and deaf individuals.
OCD	obsessive compulsive disorder	A disorder where individuals become obsessed with thoughts that reflect anxiety or fears.
OCR	Office of Civil Rights	An office that offers services and resources for civil rights.
ODAS	occupational data analysis system	A system used to identify and classify jobs in organizations.
ODD	oppositional defiant disorder	A pattern of hostile and defiant behavior.
OE	open entries	Generally refers to openings for enrollment.
OECD	Organization for Economic Cooperation and Development	Comprised of member countries that share a commitment to democratic government and market economy.
OH	orthopedically handicapped	A severe orthopedic impairment that affects an individual's educational performance.
OHI	other health impairments	Other health issues that affect a person's ability to learn, social abilities, or vocational abilities.
OMI	other minorities	Can refer to other groups of individuals considered minorities, but not for ethnic reasons.
OSEP	Office of Special Education Programs, U.S. Department of Education	An office dedicated to improving results for individuals who are under the age of twenty-one and have disabilities; a combination of several federal agencies that ensure equal access to education and promote educational excellence.
OT	occupational therapy/therapist	A professional trained to assist individuals in achieving their capacities to function in daily living activities.
OT/PT	occupational therapy/physical therapy	Therapy designed to assist individuals in achieving their capacities to function in daily living activities.
P		
P and A	protection and advocacy	Usually an agency that provides advancement in legal and human rights for individuals with disabilities.
PACER	parent advocacy coalition for educational rights center	An organization that offers resources and services to children and young adults with disabilities.

(continued)

(continued)

Acronym	What it stands for	Definition
PALS	peer-assisted learning system	A system designed to provide an individual with his or her peers to enhance learning.
PAVE	parents advocating for vocational education	An organization designed to help parents understand the educational system and how to obtain educational services for a child with special needs.
PCA	personal care attendant	Someone who assists in the care of a special-needs individual.
PCD	perceptual communicative disability	A disorder in which one or more psychological processes prevents an individual from understanding or using language in a functional way.
PDAS	professional development and appraisal system	An instrument used for appraising teachers and identifying areas that need more development.
PDD	pervasive development disorder	A broad spectrum of social and communication disorders.
PDD-NOS	pervasive development disorder—not otherwise specified	A condition in which several features of autism or other clearly identified PDD's are present.
PEATC	parent education advocacy training center	An organization that assists in training families of children with special needs as well as providing education and resources.
PECS	picture exchange communication system	An augmentative/alternative training method that teaches children and adults with autism and other communication deficits to initiate communication.
PEIMS	public education information management system	A system that contains data necessary for government agencies to perform their legal functions in regard to public education.
PEL	present education level	A determination of how the student is doing, including strengths, weaknesses, and learning style.
PERS	public employees retirement system	Provides retirement, health, and pension benefits to public employees.
PET	pupil evaluation team	Usually a team responsible for developing a service plan for a special-education student.
PIC	private industry council	A business-led organization that acts as an intermediary and connects children and adults to education and employment opportunities to meet the demands of employers.

Acronym	What it stands for	Definition
PIQ	performance IQ	Nonverbal IQ.
PLATO	programmed logic automatic teaching operations	A computer-based program often credited with being the earliest example of a virtual community.
PLI	pragmatic language impairment	A disorder that causes a child to have selective difficulties in mastering language, but to develop normally in other respects.
PLOP	present level of performance	Generally specifies the needs of the child, the strengths and weaknesses, parental concerns, and how the child's disability affects the progress in the general curriculum.
PPCD	preschool program for children with disabilities	An early childhood program designed for specific needs of children with disabilities.
PPS	pupil personnel services	Services that assist in providing an educational environment conducive to academic, personal, social, and career growth of students.
PRE-K	pre-kindergarten	School or classes for children before they enter kindergarten.
PT	physical therapy/therapist	The treatment of injuries or disorders using physical methods.
PTA	physical therapist assistant; post-traumatic amnesia; parent-teacher association	A trained assistant to a physical therapist; amnesia resulting from a concussion or other head trauma; an association comprised of parents and educators who serve as advocates for education.
PTG	parent teacher group	Groups of parents and educators who advocate for education and schools.
PTSD	post-traumatic stress disorder	A disorder that occurs following an experience of life-threatening or other traumatic events.
PTT	planning and placement team	A team that reviews a referral and plans an evaluation to determine if a student is in need of special education, and if the student is, develops and completes an IEP.
PVS	persistent vegetative state; private vocational schools	A condition of patients in whom coma has progressed to a state of wakefulness without detectable awareness; tution-based vocational school.
PY	project year	A chronological time frame for a project.

(continued)

(continued)

Acronym	What it stands for	Definition
Q		
QAFB	questions about functional behavior	An assessment that is usually given to determine someone's functional behavior.
QMRP	qualified mental retardation professional	Also known as case managers, these individuals have been trained in helping in various ways people with mental retardation.
R		
RAD	reactive attachment disorder	A disorder that causes a breakdown of social ability, usually associated with the failure to bond with a caretaker during infancy.
RCF	residential care facility	A facility where an individual is in non-medical care.
RCH	residential care home	A home where an individual is in non-medical care.
RDD	reading disorder-dyslexia	A learning disability that affects language processing and reading skills.
R&D	research & development	Research on a subject and development of solutions.
REBT	rational emotive behavior therapy	A type of psychotherapy that encourages individuals to identify negative thoughts and replace them with positive ones.
REI	regular education initiative	An initiative that advocates the integration of general and special education into one system for all students.
RFP	request for proposal	An official document that requests vendors to bid for specific products and services.
RMT	regional management team	Usually a middle management and liaison to the main organization that assesses the educational needs of a particular region, develops plans, and evaluates long-range plans as well as other duties.
RRC	regional resource centers	Usually, a center that focuses on improving programs and services for children with disabilities.
RSP	resource specialist (regional term)	A specialist that provides resources and services to families with special education.
R&T	research and training	Research in special education and training in specific areas of SE.

Acronym	What it stands for	Definition
RTC	residential treatment center	Centers that are for children who suffer from serious psychiatric disorders but are not ill enough for psychiatric hospitalization.
RTH	residential training home	A residential facility that provides training for special-needs individuals.
RTI	response to intervention	A three-step model that assesses a child's reading ability in kindergarten; introduction of scientifically based reading instruction; and if child fails to respond, the implementation of a child centered evaluation to determine what the child may need.
RWQC	regional workforce quality committee	A committee designated to facilitate the economic needs of the community and its citizens through education and training of citizens.
S		
SAT	scholastic aptitude test	An aptitude test for entry into higher education institutions.
SBE; SBOE	state board of education	The agency responsible for the state's education advocacy.
SB L-M	Stanford-Binet, Form L-M (language/memory)	A standardized psychological test to assess intelligence.
SBS	schoolwide behavior supports	A system of support that encourages positive strategies for teaching and supporting appropriate student behaviors in an effort to create positive school environments.
SDA	service delivery area	Generally refers to an area where health services are delivered and available.
SDC	special day class	A program that provides classes to students who may need more intensive support in certain academic areas.
SDE	self-directed employment	Employment in which the individual participates in all aspects of determining skills and abilities, finding a job, and maintaining the job.
SE	special education	Education that meets the special needs of students with learning disabilities or other disabilities that prevent them from participating in regular education classes.
SEA	state education agency; state education association	Each state has an education agency or association that oversees the various school districts and educational issues.

(continued)

(continued)

Acronym	What it stands for	Definition
SEAP	state education advisory panel	An advisory panel that studies and advises on various educational topics.
SECC	special education child count	A count of the children and youth, ages birth through twenty-one, who are eligible for and receiving special education and related services.
SECTION 504	see definition at right	A part of the Rehabilitation Act of 1973 making it illegal for any organization receiving federal funds to discriminate against a person solely on the basis of disability.
SED	seriously emotionally disturbed	A condition where the individual may exhibit several characteristics, such as inability to learn, inability to maintain relationships, inappropriate behavior, depression, etc.
SEMS	special education management system	Usually an automated system that supports preparation of IEP, complies with statutes, collects data, and archives.
SENCO	special education needs coordinator	An individual who helps coordinate services and provide resources to special-education students.
SENG	supporting the emotional needs of the gifted	An organization dedicated to providing gifted individuals with information, resources, guidance, and an opportunity to communicate with others in a similar situation.
SERVE	secondary education reporting of vocational enrollment	Generally, there must be documentation of a student's educational and occupational objectives when enrolling in a vocational program.
SI	speech impaired	A type of communication disorder where "normal" speech is disrupted. This can mean stuttering, lisps, vocal dysphonia, etc.
SIB	self-injurious behavior	Behavior that can cause tissue damage, such as bruises, wounds, or redness. Most common forms are head-banging, biting, and scratching.
SICC	state interagency coordinating council	This council advises agencies on what needs are not being met in early childhood special education and early intervention programs for children who have special needs. The council also reviews newly proposed rules by the state department of education, oversees the distribution of funds, and assists agencies in coordinating and participating in the statewide system.

Acronym	What it stands for	Definition
SIG	state improvement grant	A grant that usually brings together educational leaders, parents, school staff, community members, and other agencies with a common goal to improve opportunities for students with learning disabilities.
SILP	semi-independent living program	A program that emphasizes the gaining of life skills to help with a successful transition to living independently.
SIP	state improvement plan	A plan that follows the recommendations from the U.S. Department of Education Office of Special Education programs and is often used in conjunction with a state improvement grant.
SIS	shared information systems	A system that collects and preserves large amounts of information that can be shared between agencies and organizations.
SLC	structured learning center	A center designed to serve special-needs students with placement based on assessed needs outlined in the student's IEP. Services include speech pathologist, educational assistance, psychologist, and other types of therapist.
SLD	specific learning disability	Defined as a disorder in at least one of the basic psychological processes involved in language or the understanding of it; this disorder can cause problems with listening, thinking, speaking, reading, writing, and other areas.
SLP	speech-language pathologist	A professional trained to help with speech and language therapy.
SLPA	speech-language pathologist assistant	A trained assistant to a speech-language pathologist.
SLR	state liaison representative	A person who serves as an intermediary between the state and certain state agencies.
SPeNSE	study of personnel needs in special education	A study designed to address concerns about the shortages of personnel serving special-needs students and the need for qualification improvements of those employed in the field.
SOL	standards of learning	State and national expectations for student learning and achievement through twelfth grade.

(continued)

(continued)

Acronym	What it stands for	Definition
SPD	semantic pragmatic disorder	A disorder that has conflicting definitions. One opinion is that SPD is a component of some other disorders. Another opinion is that it is the same as high functioning autism or a separate disorder on the autistic spectrum.
SPED	special education	Programs designed to meet the special learning needs of individual students.
SPLD	semantic pragmatic language disorder	A component of a disorder that prevents the child from learning to speak, or speaking normally and understanding language.
SSA	social security act; SSA Social Security Administration	An act that pays benefits to those who qualify through either, age, disability, or minor issues of a deceased individual who would have otherwise received benefits; the government agency that oversees Social Security.
SSD	social security disability	A disability that allows for social security benefits.
SSDI	social security disability income	The amount of the social security benefit.
SSI	statewide systemic initiative; supplemental security income	A partnership of schools, colleges, districts, and other educational agencies that focuses on strengthening education; a federal income supplement for individuals who qualify, usually disabled individuals.
SST	student study team; student support team	School based groups that assist teachers and school staff with issues involving academic and emotional behavior problems of non-special education.
STO	short-term objective	Intermediate steps to a larger goal or benchmark.
T		
TAG	talented and gifted	Students who demonstrate an ability to learn at levels above their peers.
TBI	traumatic brain injury	Also called acquired brain injury, intracranial injury, or simply head injury, occurs when a sudden trauma causes damage to the brain. Symptoms of a TBI can be mild, moderate, or severe, depending on the extent of the damage to the brain. Outcome can be anything from complete recovery to permanent disability.

Acronym	What it stands for	Definition
TDD	telecommunication devices for the deaf	Devices that can help deaf individuals to communicate.
TESOL	teachers of English for speakers of other languages	Teachers who instruct non-English speakers.
TIP	teacher improvement process	Professional development and evaluation for teachers.
TLC	therapeutic learning center	A center that provides education and services for children with special needs in a smaller group setting with higher levels of support.
TMH	trainable mentally handicapped	A student who is moderately or severely impaired and has a reduced rate of learning.
TMR	trainably mentally retarded	Replaced by the above term.
TPP	transition planning process	A period that allows the educators and practitioners who work with special-needs individuals to acclimate them into a more independent lifestyle after school.
TOVA	test of variable attention	A test often used in determining certain types of learning disorders, like ADHD.
TTY	teletypewriter (phone system for deaf individuals—see TDD)	Devices that can help deaf individuals to communicate.
U		
UAF	university affiliated facility	A facility that is in some way associated with a particular university.
V		
VAC	vocational adjustment counselor; vocational adjustment class	A counselor who monitors the student's IEP while the student is working in his or her job; provides special education and other services to students placed on a job and have regular involvement by a special education counselor.
VCD	volitional conduct disorder	A disorder that appears to be an intentional disregard for rules and acceptable behavior.
VEDS	vocational education data systems	Derives data about vocational education primarily from existing National Center for Education Statistics (NCES) surveys.

(continued)

(continued)

Acronym	What it stands for	Definition
VI	visually impaired	Little to no useful seeing abilities.
VRD	vocational rehabilitation division	Services offered to people with disabilities and business owners to bridge work relations that benefit the community.
VSA	very special arts	An organization dedicated to using art to help rehabilitate individuals with disabilities.
W		
WAC	work activity center	A center that uses alternative training method to train people with disabilities to become active and independent workers.
WISC-R	Weschler Intelligence Scale for Children-Revised	Intelligence tests that use age-appropriate word-based activities and mechanical, puzzle-like activities to test problem-solving skills.
WISC-III	Weschler Intelligence Scale for Children-Third Edition	Intelligence tests that use age-appropriate word-based activities and mechanical, puzzle-like activities to test problem-solving skills; this version often used to determine potential learning disabilities.
WOD	written output disorder	A disorder that can cause slow, labored, and illegible writing. Can be caused by numerous disabilities.
WQC	workplace quality council	A council that monitors and advocates for an overall healthy workplace environment.
WRAP	wraparound program	Wraparound is an approach to use individualized, comprehensive services for youth with complicated multi-dimensional problems.
Y		
YTP	youth transition program	Generally, a collaborative effort between agencies to design and improve school-to-work transitions for special-needs students.

THE FORMS

Sample Form #1: Individualized Family Service Plan

Cover

The cover is optional for families to complete.

The cover of the Individualized Family Service Plan (IFSP) provides a way for the family to record important information about the child enrolled in North Carolina's Infant-Toddler Program. It emphasizes the family's ownership of the Individualized Family Service Plan (IFSP).

The family is encouraged to personalize the cover as they choose, perhaps writing their child's name in a star space or having an older child decorate the page. A photograph or a poem is another way of decorating this page. The cover should reflect the family's individuality and what makes them feel good.

Important Dates and Events

There are important dates and events in the lives of all families. Space is available to write in dates and events that are important to the family and their child's development. The family is encouraged to use this space to indicate important dates and events. Examples might be the achievement of developmental milestones, evaluations, and the start of a new service.

I. Individualized Family Service Plan (IFSP) information

Child's Name: _____

Parent(s') Name(s): _____

_____

Address: _____

_____

City/State: _____

Day Phone: _____

Evening Phone: _____

County: _____

ZIP Code: _____

Date of Birth: _____

Age at Referral: _____

Date of Referral: _____

Interim IFSP Date: _____

IFSP Date: _____

Table A.D.1.   IFSP Team

Name	Relationship/ Role	Phone Number	Address	Date

Rev. 02/01 IFSP/DEIE

Language Spoken at Home: _____

School District: _____

Soc. Sec. No.: _____

Child's Name: _____

Record Number: _____

Agency Code: _____

Section Number: _____

I. Individualized Family Service Plan (IFSP) Information

The information section includes specific data about the child and family. It also has space for listing the IFSP team members. This section can serve as a directory for the team members.

Child's Name: Enter the first, middle, and last name of the child.

Parent's Name: Enter the name(s) of parent(s) or guardian.

Address: Enter street, route, or post office box address(es) of parent(s) or guardian.

City/State: Record city and state.

Day Phone: Enter phone number where parent(s) can be reached during the day.

Evening Phone: Enter phone number where parent(s) can be reached during the evening.

County: Enter the child's legal county of residence.

ZIP Code: Record ZIP code.

Date of Birth: Enter month/day/year of child's birth.

Sex: Enter "M" for male and "F" for female.

Age at Referral: Enter child's chronological age at time of referral to the Infant-Toddler Program.

Date of Referral: Enter month/day/year the child was referred to the Infant-Toddler Program.

Interim IFSP Date: If this document is an interim IFSP enter the month/day/year the family signs. Otherwise, enter "NA".

IFSP Date: Enter the month/day/year the family signs the IFSP.

IFSP Team: List the family members' names to be followed by the Child Service Coordinator and other team members. Include guardians, foster, and surrogate parents as team members. Enter the name of the team member, the relationship/role, the phone number, the address, and the date the team member began working with the family.

Language Spoken in Home: Enter the language(s) spoken by the primary caregivers in the home where the child lives.

School District: Enter the school or school district in which the child's current address is located.

Soc. Sec. No.: Enter the child's Social Security Number.

Child's Name: Enter the first, middle, and last name of the child.

Record Number: Enter your agency's designated record number for the child.

Agency Code: (OPTIONAL) Enter a code identifying your agency, if desired.

II. Family's Concerns, Priorities, and Resources
(*Optional: for the family to complete*) Why are you interested in receiving help for your child?

What do you want the IFSP Team to know about your child?
    Pregnancy and birth history
    History of child's growth and development
    Medical information
    Other important events or information
    When you were first concerned
    Effect of child's needs on the family
    Child likes
    Family activities
    Parent choices
    Your concerns now
    What is most important to you now
    Helpful people and agencies

Date	Information

Rev. 02/01 IFSP/DEIE

Child's Name: _____

Record Number: _____

Agency Code: _____

Section Number: _____

II. Family's Concerns, Priorities, and Resources

This section is optional for families to complete.

Including family information in the IFSP is voluntary on the part of the family. This information helps identify what families want from early intervention for their children and themselves.

It is important for the family to express their concerns, priorities, and resources in a positive manner because these elements become the backbone for the rest of the document. This section should be presented to families to complete. Staff should be available to assist by lending encouragement, giving examples, brainstorming, etc. In some instances the Child Service Coordinator may be requested or need to offer to record the family's concerns, priorities, and resources.

Why are you interested in receiving help for your child?

This question is asked because it encourages the family to express their hopes for growth and change. Families may not know what services are available and might respond, "We are not sure; our doctor suggested we come and talk with you." Regardless of the response, it opens discussion and the opportunity to express concerns.

What do you want the team to know about your child?

This section suggests topics for the family to address, and gives them the freedom to choose what they wish to address. The topics are only there to generate discussion and do not pertain to all situations. This is where the family shares their perspective of events in their child's life. Information may point out areas where strengths can be reinforced or assistance is needed. In recounting their stories, families often find new ways of seeing events and recognizing strengths.

If the family elects not to complete this section, the Child Service Coordinator should document on the page that the opportunity was offered and declined at this time.

Date: Use this column to indicate the date the family shares concerns, priorities, and resources and other information.

Information: Record information related by the family pertaining to their concerns, priorities, and resources and other information.

III. Summary of Child's Present Abilities and Strengths
Include a summary of functional assessments, evaluations, and observations of the child in his day-to-day environment. List evaluators, procedures, results, and child's strengths and needs. Address all of the following domains for an initial IFSP.

Adaptive/self help skills (bathing, feeding, dressing, toileting, etc.)

Cognitive skills (thinking, reasoning, learning)

Communication skills (responding, understanding, and using language)

Physical development (vision, hearing, motor, and health)

Social/emotional skills (feelings, playing, and interacting)

Date	Description

Rev. 02/01 IFSP/DEIE

Child's Name: _____

Record Number: _____

Agency Code: _____

Section Number: _____

III. Summary of Child's Present Abilities and Strengths

In this section the results of all evaluations are summarized and discussed by the team for the initial IFSP. Each domain must be addressed for the initial IFSP. It includes the family's observations of the child in his day-to-day environments, medical information, formal evaluations, and other sources of information. The team includes the parent(s), as well as other professionals representing several disciplines, and the Child Service Coordinator. The summary information should be written in simple jargon-free language so that it is clear and understandable to all.

Emphasis should be given to a child's present abilities and strengths in day-to-day life rather than on developmental levels. This is particularly important since many evaluations compare a child's development to the development of children without disabilities. This section includes information on what the child can do and what he needs to learn. The child's learning style is also described so that natural abilities can be strengthened and built upon. New information about the child's abilities, strengths, and needs should be added as evaluations, assessments, and observations are conducted.

Date: Enter the date the evaluation(s), assessment(s), or observation(s) took place.

Description: The summary of the team evaluation must include names of evaluators/their titles, assessments used, and statements that describe the child's present status and levels of development in all of the following domains for the initial IFSP:

1. Adaptive/self-help skills (bathing, feeding, dressing, toileting, etc.)
2. Cognitive skills (thinking, reasoning, learning)
3. Communication skills (responding, understanding, and using language)
4. Physical development (vision, hearing, motor, and current health status)
5. Social/emotional skills (feelings, playing, interacting)

IV. IFSP Outcomes

Family's Concerns, Priorities, and Resources	Child's Abilities/Needs

Outcome No._____   Start Date_____   Target Date

_____

_____

_____

Activities			Person Responsible

Date Reviewed	Outcome Status	Comments on Status	Child's Name
			_____
			Record Number
			_____
			Agency Code
			_____
			Section Number
			_____

IV. IFSP Outcomes

Outcomes are the changes the family wants for themselves or for their child. Outcomes should be discussed at the IFSP meeting by all team members as related to the family's concerns, priorities, and resources; the child's abilities and needs; or both. New outcomes can be added at any time additions are desired or needed by the families.

Family's Concerns, Priorities, and Resources: State the family's concerns along with their priorities and resources when related to the identified outcome.

Concerns are the areas identified by the family as needs, issues, or problems they want to address.

Priorities are things or accomplishments important to the family.

Resources are formal and informal means that can help the family.

Child's Abilities/Needs: State what the child is able to do and what he needs to be able to do when related to the identified outcome.

Outcome No._____: Place the sequential number of the outcome on the line. Then in the space provided write a description of the desired end result of what the child or family will do or accomplish. Each subsequent outcome should be numbered consecutively per page in Section IV. Outcomes may be child- or family-focused.

Target Date: Enter the anticipated date this outcome will be completed. The target date may be left blank at the request of the family. Enter revised target dates as needed when time frames must be adjusted.

Start Date: Enter the date that work toward the desired outcome will begin.

Activities: Describe the methods and procedures that will be used to reach the outcome. Include a projected completion date if desired. Activities should tell the person reading the statement what is being done to achieve the outcome.

Person Responsible: Name the person(s) responsible for carrying out the activities to help the child or family achieve the outcome. Family member(s) may be identified as person(s) responsible.

Dates Reviewed/Outcome Status/Comments: Enter the date outcome progress was reviewed. Next to the date, write one of these terms: "achieved, ongoing, discontinued" to describe outcome status at that time. Under comments, explain why an outcome is ongoing or discontinued. Additional review dates and outcome status should be entered as appropriate if prior review status was "ongoing."

V. IFSP Service Delivery Plan

Service	Provider	Start Date	Location/ Most Natural Environment	Fre- quency/ Intensity	Cost to Family/ Payment Arrange- ment	Antici- pated Duration	Date Ended	Parent/ Coordi- native Agency Signatures

Child's Name: _____

Record Number: _____

Agency Code: _____

Section Number: _____

V. IFSP Service Delivery Plan

The IFSP Service Delivery Plan is intended to help identify important details in carrying out the activities written in the IFSP Outcomes Section IV. The IFSP Service Delivery Plan provides a way to record specific information to explain how, when, where, and under what conditions the services are expected.

Family members and professionals are encouraged to discuss services openly and to make joint decisions based on the outcomes chosen by the parents or family members. The services should be provided by qualified individuals in the child's natural environment as much as possible. The cost for services to family members is an important matter to be considered in planning services. Use cost information that is available. Expectations about how long the services will be provided are another detail to be discussed. Reaching agreement will help all who have a responsibility identified in the plan to meet family members' and providers' expectations.

Service: Record the type of service planned. Consider both recommended and required services.

Required services are:

- Assistive Technology Services and Devices
- Audiological Services
- Child Service Coordination
- Early Identification and Screening
- Family Counseling and Therapy Services
- Health Services
- Medical Services
- Multidisciplinary Evaluations and Assessments
- Nursing Services
- Nutrition Services

- Occupational Therapy

- Physical Therapy

- Psychological Services

- Respite Services

- Social Work Services

- Special Instruction

- Speech-Language Therapy

- Transportation

- Vision Services

Provider: Record the agency/organization that will provide the service.

Start Date: Record the month, day, and year the service is planned to begin.

Location/Most Natural Environment: Record the actual place or places where the service will be provided. To the maximum extent appropriate to the needs of the child, Early Intervention services must be provided in natural environments including the home and community settings where children without disabilities participate. If the most natural environment is not utilized, indicate this in the column, explain the reason why, and describe briefly why the specific setting was chosen.

Frequency/Intensity: Record the number of days or sessions that a service will be provided (e.g., four times a month, once quarterly, two times per week), the length of each session, and whether the service is on an individual or group basis. Child Service Coordination should be provided based on the intensity of family need, but numbers of approximate frequency and intensity should be stated.

Cost to Family/Payment Arrangement: If known, record the approximate cost of the service to the child's family. The cost is the amount the family will be obligated to pay. The estimated cost should be based on the usual and customary fees charged by the provider and excludes amounts expected to be covered by insurance and sliding-scale fee allowances. Put "none" if there is no cost to the family. Sources of payment typically are one or more of the following:

- Private insurance
- Self-payment
- Medicaid
- Other public or private resources

Parent/Coordinative Agency Signatures: This column should not be completed unless changes occur after the initial IFSP is signed. Parent(s) or guardian(s) signify agreement with any changes in services by signing in this column. Coordinative Agencies or Designees sign this column when there is an increase in intensity or frequency of a service or a new service is added.

Anticipated Duration: Record the month, day, and year that represents how long the service is expected to occur.

Date Ended: Record the month, day, and year the service was completed.

VI. Parent/Coordinative Agency Agreement

- ☐ I have participated in developing this Individualized Family Service Plan (IFSP).

- ☐ I have been fully informed about all the services and costs involved.

- ☐ I understand it is my choice to accept this plan and I can change my mind at any time.

- ☐ I understand all team members and coordinative agencies may get a copy of this IFSP.

- ☐ I agree for my child and family to receive the services outlined in this IFSP except as noted below.

☐ I have been fully informed of my rights under the Infant-Toddler Program.

Comments/concerns I wish to add:

Parent/Guardian Signature: _____

Date _____

Parent/Guardian Signature: _____

Date: _____

Other Signature: _____

Date: _____

Other Signature: _____

Date: _____

☐ I agree to work with the family and local service providers to ensure availability of services as listed in this IFSP.

Service Coordinator Signature/Agency: _____

Date: _____

Coordinative Agency or Designee Signature/Agency: _____

Date: _____

Coordinative Agency or Designee Signature/Agency: _____

Date: _____

Coordinative Agency or Designee Signature/Agency: _____

Date: _____

Child's Name: _____

Record Number: _____

Agency Code: _____

Section Number: _____

VI. Parent/Coordinative Agency Agreement

The family is a consumer of Early Intervention services and should be involved in developing the IFSP. The contents of the IFSP must be fully explained, and the agreement statement must be reviewed. The parent or guardian should be informed that his signature will indicate:

- Participation in developing the plan

- Advisement on all services and costs involved

- Choice to accept or reject plan

- Right to change mind at any time

- Awareness of IFSP distribution

- Agreement with the plan

Comments/concerns I wish to add: The parent may record any additional information, concerns, or differences. The parent may wish to comment as to the distribution of optional pages to the team members and coordinative agencies.

Signatures: The parent's or guardian's legal rights are recognized by asking for his signature. The parent or guardian signs and dates where indicated. The Child Service Coordinator and Coordinative Agency Representatives or their Designees sign and date where indicated acknowledging their agreement to work with the family and service providers to ensure the availability of services listed in this IFSP.

A Coordinative Agency need only sign this agreement when services are being listed for which the agency has coordinative responsibility. If these are listed when the IFSP is developed, the Coordinative Agency signs then and subsequently initials later any increases on the IFSP

Service Delivery Plan [Section V]. If a Coordinative Agency has no services listed when an IFSP is first developed, but services are added later, then the Coordinative Agency signature is obtained at the time services are added. If an additional service for which the Coordinative Agency has responsibility is added after the signing of the IFSP, then the Coordinative Agency initials the IFSP Service Delivery Plan [Section V] to acknowledge the added service. Service providers may sign *but are not required to do so.*

VII. IFSP Review

Review Date	Summarize Review Results
REVIEW CYCLE O Semi-Annual O Annual O Other	
	Target Date for Next Review _____

I have participated in the review of this IFSP. The rights under the Infant-Toddler Program have been reviewed and explained. The latest copy of the Parent Handbook for the Infant-Toddler Program has been given.

Parent/Guardian Signature: _____

Date: _____

Signature/Agency Child Service Coordinator Signature:

_____

Date _____

Child's Name: _____

Record Number: _____

Agency Code: _____

Section Number: _____

VII. IFSP Review

This section is to be used any time there is an IFSP review. It is not necessary to wait until a Semi-Annual or Annual Review to review the plan and make changes that are needed or desired by the family. Three (3) kinds of IFSP reviews are:

• Semi-annual

• Annual

• Other reviews (at the family's request)

Review Date: Enter the month, day, and year the review takes place.

Summarize Review Results: There are times when reviews are not conducted as scheduled. If this should occur, note the reasons why a review is not conducted on schedule. If the family forgoes the review, the Child Service Coordinator should convene a review meeting with the other service providers to document that the review has occurred. The family and service providers are encouraged to make comments in this section related to:

• Progress being made toward achieving outcomes

• The family's satisfaction with services being received

• Any new and relevant information related to the child and family

- The results of any evaluations and assessments conducted
- Plans until the next scheduled review
- At Annual Review, whether this IFSP will continue or a new IFSP will be developed
- Team members who were present
- How team members not present contributed to the review

Review Cycle: Check the space that corresponds to the kind of review. Use a new Section VII every time there is a review.

Target Date for Next Review: Record the date when the next review will be conducted. A review of the IFSP is to occur every six months following the date of the signing of the Initial IFSP. If a review is delayed, the next review should occur on schedule from the date of the signing of the Initial IFSP, even if a full six months has not elapsed.

Signatures: Enter the signatures of the Child Service Coordinator, the parents, and the parent surrogates who are present at the review meeting. A parent signature indicates receipt of the latest copy of the Parent Handbook for the Infant-Toddler Program and that the rights under this program have been reviewed and explained. Others participating in the review may sign if they desire.

Sample Form #2

Individualized Family Service Plan

Child's Name: _____ Birth Date: _____

Date of IFSP: _____ Child's Gender: _____ Race/Ethnicity: _____

Eligibility Reason: _____

Primary Language: _____

Service Coordinator: _____

Section A: Family Considerations for the IFSP

1. Please describe how you see your child (what you like, any concerns or needs).

2. What special skills does your family have in meeting your child's needs?

3. Which of the following do you or other family members feel are important concerns or areas about which you would like more information and/or assistance?

For your child:		For your family:
☐ Getting around	☐ Meeting other families whose child has similar needs/support group	☐ Child care
☐ Communicating	☐ Finding or working with doctors or other specialists	☐ Finding or working with people who can help you in the home or care for your child so you can have a break
☐ Learning	☐ Coordinating your child's medical care	☐ Housing, clothing, jobs, food, telephone
☐ Feeding, nutrition	☐ Finding out more about how different services work or how they could work better for you	☐ Family training
☐ Having fun with other children	☐ Planning or expectations for the future	☐ Brothers, sisters, friends, relatives, others
☐ Challenging behaviors or emotions	☐ Information about other available resources	☐ Information about the disability or diagnosis
☐ Equipment or supplies	☐ Transportation	☐ Money for extra costs of child's special needs
☐ Health or dental care	☐ Help with insurance/SSI/Medicade	☐ Recreation
☐ Pain or discomfort	☐ Other	
☐ Vision or hearing		
☐ Other		

1. What else do you think would be helpful for others to know about your child and family?

2. Are there other concerns you would like to discuss?

Section B: All About Our Child

My Name: _____

My Nickname: _____

Things I like to do	People I am with (names, ages, amount of time)
____ Take naps	In my home:
____ Ride in a car	
____ Play outside	
____ Daycare/play group	At my day care:
____ Eat out	
____ Listen to music	
____ Grocery shopping	With my friends:
____ Church/religious practice	
____ Play with family members	
____ Play with other children	With neighbors, relatives:
____ Play in water/take a bath	
____ Watch/listen to TV	

Section C: All About Our Family

Who is in our family:

People who are important to our family: (relatives, neighbors, friends, doctors)

Things we like to do as a family:

About our neighborhood, our community:

Section D: Child's Developmental Status

Statement of child's functioning in the areas of cognitive development, physical development, communication development, social and emotional development, and adaptive development:

Area	Test/Obs. Used	Tester/Observer/Date	Chron. Age/Adj. Age	Age Level/Age Range
Cognitive				
Communication				
Physical Development				
Social/Emotional				
Adaptive				
Other				

Statement of child's current health status including vision and hearing:

Other relevant birth history, health history, medical diagnosis, family medical history, nutrition status, etc.

Section E: Major Outcomes

Major outcome to be achieved:
What's happening now?
How will we know when we're making progress?

Activities/Strategies (Things we'll do to achieve this outcome)	Resources/People (who will teach, learn, or do)	Location	Date and Family's Evaluation

Family's Evaluation Ratings:

1. Situation changed, no longer a need

2. Situation unchanged, still a need, goal, or project

3. Implementation begun, still a need, goal, or project

4. Outcome partially attained or accomplished

5. Outcome accomplished or attained, but not to the family's satisfaction

6. Outcome mostly accomplished or attained to the family's satisfaction

7. Outcome completely accomplished or attained to the family's satisfaction

Section F: Service Settings/Natural Environment

To the extent appropriate, Early Intervention services must be provided in the types of settings in which infants and toddlers without delays and their families would participate:

Check all sites to be considered as OPTIONS for Early Intervention services in your community:

- ☐ Child's home
- ☐ Other family location
- ☐ Family day care
- ☐ Community-based program:
- ☐ Child care program
    - ☐ Head Start
    - ☐ Play group
    - ☐ Other: _____
- ☐ Early Intervention classroom/center
- ☐ Hospital/clinic
- ☐ Other: _____

Indicate and describe below any changes necessary to permit successful accommodation of and programming for the child in the most natural setting (e.g., adaptations in rooms or environment, transportation, materials, equipment, technology, techniques or methods, curriculum, staff training, etc.)

Describe accommodations to be used in ALL sites to promote successful participation:

Describe additional accommodations which are site-specific; indicate at which sites they are needed and why:

Section G: Early Intervention Services

Intervention Service	Provider	Location	Method Individual = I Group = G	Frequency/ Intensity	Initiation Date	Duration (Months)

Location:

1. Home
2. Family day care
3. Regular nursery/day-care center
4. Outpatient service facility
5. E.I. class/center
6. Hospital (inpatient)

7. Residential facility

8. Other setting

Frequency: Number of times per week/month
Intensity: Length of session
Early Intervention service options include:

Assistive Technology	Nursing Service	Social Work
Audiological Services	Nutrition Services	Special Instruction
Family Training	Counseling	Home Visits
Health Services	Occupational Therapy	Speech/Language
Physical Therapy	Transportation	Vision Services
Psychological Services	Medical Diagnostic Services	Service Coordination*

*Service coordination is required for all children.

Section H: Transition Planning Checklist

Transition Plan Provisions	Date Initiated	Comments/Person Responsible
Discuss community program options for child		
Discuss community program options for family		
Discuss parental rights and responsibilities under Part B providing information on resources and advocacy groups		
Identify and implement steps to assist families in evaluating available and eligible programs and services		
Transmit specified information to other community programs, upon parent request		
Transmit specified information to local education agency with written consent from parents		
Identify and implement steps to help child and family adjust to and function in new environments		

Transition plan comments:

Section I: Family Service Planning Team

IFSP Meeting Participants: The following individuals participated in the development of this IFSP:

Name	Title/Role	Agency

IEP SAMPLE FORM

Exhibit C.1. Annotated IEP Checklist

Item(s)	IDEA '97 Regulations	Regulation Citation
Parent/Student—IEP 1		
☐ Consider input from parents	Parent participation	20 U.S.C § 614 (d) (1) (B) (i)
Student Strengths and Key Evaluation Summary—IEP 1		
☐ Consider results of initial evaluation or most recent evaluation	Initial evaluations Reevaluation IEP meetings Development, review, and revision of IEP	20 U.S.C § 614 (a) (b) and (c) 20 U.S.C § 614 (a) (2) 20 U.S.C § 613 (a) (1); 614 (d) (4) (A) 20 U.S.C § 614 (d) (3) and (4) (B) and (e)
☐ Consider assessment results from MCAS and districtwide assessments	Development, review, and revision of IEP	20 U.S.C § 614 (d) (3) and (4) (B) and (e)
☐ Consider input from parents, special educators, and general education teachers	IEP meetings Parent participation Development, review, and revision of IEP	20 U.S.C § 613 (a) (1); 614 (d) (4) (A) 20 U.S.C § 614 (d) (1) (B) (i) 20 U.S.C § 614 (d) (3) and (4) (B) and (e)
☐ Review existing annual goals and address any lack of expected progress	IEP meetings	20 U.S.C § 613 (a) (1); 614 (d) (4) (A)
☐ Review progress in the general curriculum	IEP meetings	20 U.S.C § 613 (a) (1); 614 (d) (4) (A)
Vision Statement—IEP 1		
☐ Beginning at age 14, the vision statement should be based on the individual student's needs, taking into account the student's preferences and interests, and include desired outcomes in adult living, postsecondary, and working environments	Transition services Development, review, and revision of IEP	20 U.S.C § 614 (d) (1) (A) (i) (VIII) 20 U.S.C § 614 (d) (3) and (4) (B) and (e)

(continued)

Exhibit C.1. Annotated IEP Checklist *(continued)*

General Curriculum—IEP 2		
☐ Discuss how the student's disability affects the student's involvement and progress in the general curriculum (i.e., the same curriculum used with nondisabled students)	Content of IEP	20 U.S.C § 614 (d) (1) (A) and (d) (6) (A) (ii)

Massachusetts DOE/Annotated IEP Checklist—REVISED (4/23/01) CKL 1		
Item(s)	**Idea '97 Regulations**	**Regulation Citation**
Other Educational Need(s)—IEP 3		
☐ For the student whose behavior impedes own learning or the learning of others, consider student's behavior, including positive behavioral interventions, ability to follow school discipline code, any needed code modifications, and the possible need for a functional behavioral assessment	Development, review, and revision of IEP	20 U.S.C § 614 (d) (3) and (4) (B) and (e)
☐ For the student with Limited English Proficient (LEP), consider language needs and document whether the special education and related services will be provided in a language other than English	Development, review, and revision of IEP	20 U.S.C § 614 (d) (3) and (4) (B) and (e)
☐ For the student who is blind/visually impaired, consider the need for instruction in Braille and the use of Braille, unless the Team considers such instruction is not appropriate for the student	Development, review, and revision of IEP	20 U.S.C § 614 (d) (3) and (4) (B) and (e)
☐ For the student who is deaf/hearing impaired, consider language and communication needs, opportunities for direct communication, academic level, and full range of needs, including direct instruction in a child's language and communication mode	Development, review, and revision of IEP	20 U.S.C § 614 (d) (3) and (4) (B) and (e)
☐ For all students, consider the communication needs	Development, review, and revision of IEP	20 U.S.C § 614 (d) (3) and (4) (B) and (e)

☐ For all students, consider whether assistive technology is needed	Assistive technology Development, review, and revision of IEP	20 U.S.C § 614 (d) (3) (B) (v) 20 U.S.C § 614 (d) (3) and (4) (B) and (e)
☐ For children ages 3 to 5, consider, as appropriate, how the disability(ies) affects the child's participation in appropriate activities *Note: By the third birthday of a child eligible for services, an IEP or IESP must be developed and being implemented.*	Content of the IEP *Individualized family service plan* *Free appropriate public education (FAPE)* *Transition of children from Part C to preschool programs* *When IEPs must be in effect*	20 U.S.C § 614 (d) (1) (A) and (d) (6) (A) (ii) 20 U.S.C § 636 (d) 20 U.S.C § 612 (a) (1) 20 U.S.C § 612 (a) (9) 20 U.S.C § 614 (d) (2)
☐ Beginning no later than the first IEP developed when the eligible student with a disability is 15, the Team considers the student's need for transition services and documents their discussion. If appropriate, the IEP includes a statement of needed transition services.	Transition Services Parent participation Content of the IEP	20 U.S.C § 614 (d) (1) (A) (i) (VIII) 20 U.S.C § 614 (d) (1) (B) (i) 20 U.S.C § 614 (d) (1) (A) and (d) (6) (A) (ii)

School District Name:
School District Address:
School District Contact:
Person/Phone No.:

Individualized Education Program

IEP Dates: from _____ to _____

Student Name: _____ DOB: _____ ID No.: _____ Grade/Level: _____

Parent and/or Student Concerns

What concern(s) does the parent and/or student want to see addressed in this IEP to enhance the student's education?

Student Strengths and Key Evaluation Results Summary

What are the student's educational strengths, interest areas, significant personal attributes and personal accomplishments? What is the student's type of disability(ies), general education performance, including MCAS/district test results, achievement toward goals, and lack of expected progress, if any?

(continued)

Exhibit C.1. Annotated IEP Checklist *(continued)*

Vision Statement: What is the vision for this student?
Consider the next 1- to 5-year period when developing this statement. Beginning no later than age 14, the statement should be based on the student's preferences and interest, and should include desired outcomes in adult living, postsecondary, and working environments.

IEP Dates: from _____ to _____

Student Name: _____ DOB: _____ ID No.: _____

Present Levels of Educational Performance
A: General Curriculum

Check all that apply.

General curriculum area(s) affected by this student's disability(ies):

☐ English Language Arts — Consider the language, composition, literature (including reading), and media strands.

☐ History and Social Sciences — Consider the history, geography, economics, and civics and government strands.

☐ Science and Technology — Consider the inquiry, domains of science, technology and science, and technology and human affairs strands.

☐ Mathematics — Consider the number sense, patterns, relations and functions, geometry and measurement and statistics and probability strands.

☐ Other Curriculum Areas — Specify:

How does the disability(ies) affect progress in the curriculum area(s)?

What type(s) of accommodation, *if any*, is necessary for the student to make effective progress?

What type(s) of specially designed instruction, *if any*, is necessary for the student to make effective progress?
Check the necessary instructional modification(s) and describe how such modification(s) will be made.
☐ Content:
☐ Methodology/Delivery of Instruction:
☐ Performance Criteria:

Individualized Education Program

IEP Dates: from _____ to _____

Student Name: _____ DOB: _____ ID #.: _____

Present Levels of Educational Performance
B: Other Educational Needs

Check all that apply.

☐ Adapted physical education

☐ Assistive tech devices/services

☐ Communication (deaf/hard of hearing students)

☐ Braille needs (blind/visually impaired)

☐ Communication (all students)

☐ Nonacademic activities

☐ Extra curriculum activities

☐ Language needs (LEP students)

☐ Skill development related to vocational preparation or experience

☐ Social/emotional needs

☐ Travel training

☐ General Considerations

☐ Behavior

Age-Specific Considerations

☐ For children ages 3 to 5—participation in appropriate activities

☐ For children ages 14+ (or younger if appropriate)—student's course of study

☐ For children ages 16 (or younger if appropriate) to 22—transition to post-school activities including community experiences, employment objectives, other post school adult living and, if appropriate, daily living skills

How does the disability(ies) affect progress in the indicated area(s) of other educational needs?

What type(s) of accommodation, *if any*, is necessary for the student to make effective progress?

What type(s) of specially designed instruction, *if any*, is necessary for the student to make effective progress?
Check the necessary instructional modification(s) and describe how such modification(s) will be made.

☐ Content:

☐ Methodology/Delivery of Instruction:

☐ Performance Criteria:

Individualized Education Program

Student Name: _____

IEP Dates: from _____ to _____

DOB: _____ ID No.: _____

Current Performance Levels/Measurable Annual Goals

Goal	Specific Goal

Current Performance Level: What can the student currently do?

Measurable Annual Goal: What challenging, yet attainable, goal can we expect the student to meet by the end of this IEP period? How will we know that the student has reached this goal?

Benchmark/Objectives: What will the student need to do to complete this goal?

Goal	Specific Goal

Current Performance Level: What can the student currently do?

Measurable Annual Goal: What challenging, yet attainable, goal can we expect the student to meet by the end of this IEP period? How will we know that the student has reached this goal?

Benchmark/Objectives: What will the student need to do to complete this goal?

Progress reports are required to be sent to parents at least as often as parents are informed of their nondisabled children's progress. Each progress report must describe the student's progress toward meeting each annual goal.

Individualized Education Program

IEP Dates: from _____ to _____

Student Name: _____ DOB: _____ ID No.: _____

Service Delivery

What are the total service-delivery needs of this student?

Include services, related services, program modifications and supports (including positive behavioral supports, school personnel, and/or parent training/supports). Services should assist the student in reaching IEP goals, being involved and progressing in the general curriculum, participating in extracurricular/nonacademic activities, and allowing the student to participate with nondisabled students while working toward IEP goals.

School District   ☐ 5-day   ☐ 6-day   ☐ 10-day   ☐ other:
Cycle: cycle   cycle   cycle

A. Consultation (Indirect Services to School Personnel and Parents)

Focus on Goal No.	Type of Service	Type of Personnel	Frequency and Duration/Per Cycle	Start Date	End Date

B. Special Education and Related Services in General Education Classroom (Direct Service)

Focus on Goal No.	Type of Service	Type of Personnel	Frequency and Duration/Per Cycle	Start Date	End Date

(continued)

Exhibit C.1. Annotated IEP Checklist *(continued)*

C. Special Education and Related Services in Other Settings (Direct Service)					
Focus on Goal No.	Type of Service	Type of Personnel	Frequency and Duration/Per Cycle	Start Date	End Date

Individualized Education Program

Student Name: _____

IEP Dates: from _____ to _____

DOB: _____   ID #.: _____

Nonparticipation Justification

Is the student removed from the general education classroom at any time? (Refer to IEP 5—Service Delivery, Section C.)

☐   ☐   If yes, why is removal considered critical to the student's program?
No   Yes

IDEA 2004 Regulation 20 U.S.C. §612 (a) (5).550: "... removal of children with disabilities from the regular educational environment occurs **only when** the nature or severity of the disability of a child is such that education in regular classes with the use of supplementary aids and services cannot be achieved satisfactorily." *(Emphasis added.)*

Schedule Modification
Shorter: Does this student require a *shorter school day or shorter school year?*
☐ No   ☐ Yes—shorter day   ☐ Yes—shorter year   If yes, answer the questions below.

Longer: Does this student require a longer school day or a longer school year to prevent substantial loss of previously learned skills and/or substantial difficulty in relearning skills?
☐ No   ☐ Yes—longer day   ☐ Yes—longer year   If yes, answer the questions below.

How will the student's schedule be modified? Why is this schedule modification being recommended?
If a longer day or year is recommended, how will the school district coordinate services across program components?

Transportation Services
Does the student require transportation as a result of the disability(ies)?
☐   Regular transportation will be provided in the same manner as it would be provided for students without disabilities.
No   If the child is placed away from the local school, transportation will be provided.

☐   Special transportation will be provided in the following manner:
    ☐   On a regular transportation vehicle with the following modifications and/or specialized equipment and precautions:
    ☐   On a special transportation vehicle with the following modifications and/or specialized equipment and precautions:

After the team makes a transportation decision and after a placement decision has been made, a parent may choose to provide transportation and may be eligible for reimbursement under certain circumstances. Any parent who plans to transport their child to school should notify the school district contact person.

Individualized Education Program

IEP Dates: from _____ to _____

Student Name: _____ DOB: _____ ID No.: _____

State or Districtwide Assessment

Identify state or districtwide assessments planned during this IEP period:

Fill out the table below. Consider any state or districtwide assessment to be administered during the time span covered by this IEP. For each content area, identify the student's assessment participation status by putting an "X" in the corresponding box for column 1, 2, or 3.

	1. Assessment participation: Student participates in on-demand testing under routine conditions in this content area.	2. Assessment participation: Student participates in on-demand testing with accommodations in this content area. (See[1] below)	3. Assessment participation: Student participates in alternative assessment in this content area. (See[2] below)
CONTENT AREAS	**COLUMN 1**	**COLUMN 2**	**COLUMN 3**
English Language Arts	☐	☐	☐
History and Social Sciences	☐	☐	☐
Mathematics	☐	☐	☐
Science and Technology	☐	☐	☐
Reading	☐	☐	☐

[1]For each content area identified by an "X" in column 2 above: note in the space below, the content area and describe the accommodations necessary for participation in the on-demand testing. Any accommodations used for assessment purposes should be closely modeled on the accommodations that are provided to the student as part of his/her instructional program.

(continued)

Exhibit C.1.   Annotated IEP Checklist *(continued)*

[2] For each content area identified by an X in column 3 above: note in the space below, the content area, why the on-demand assessment is not appropriate, and how that content area will be alternatively assessed. Make sure to include the learning standards that will be addressed in each content area, the recommended assessment method(s), and the recommended evaluation and reporting method(s) for the student's performance on the alternative assessment.

> **NOTE**
>
> When state model(s) for alternative assessments are adopted, the district may enter use of state model(s) for how content area(s) will be assessed.

Individualized Education Program

IEP Dates: from _____ to _____

Student Name: _____   DOB: _____ ID No.: _____

Additional Information

☐ Include the following transition information: the anticipated graduation date; a statement of interagency responsibilities or needed linkages; the discussion of transfer of rights at least one year before age of majority; and a recommendation for Chapter 688 Referral.

☐ Document efforts to obtain participation if a parent and if student did not attend meeting or provide input.

☐ Record other relevant IEP information not previously stated.

Response Section

School Assurance

I certify that the goals in this IEP are those recommended by the Team and that the indicated services will be provided.

Signature and Role of LEA Representative   Date

Parent Options/Responses

It is important that the district knows your decision as soon as possible. Please indicate your response by checking at least one (1) box and returning a signed copy to the district. Thank you.

☐ I accept the IEP as developed.   ☐ I reject the IEP as developed.

☐ I reject the following portions of the IEP with the understanding that any portion(s) that I do not reject will be considered accepted and implemented immediately. Rejected portions are as follows:

_____

_____

_____

_____

☐ I request a meeting to discuss the rejected IEP or rejected portion(s).

Signature of Parent, Guardian, Educational Surrogate Parent, Student 18 and Over*

Date
Required signature once a student reaches 18 unless there is a court-appointed guardian.

Parent Comment: I would like to make the following comment(s) but realize any comment(s) made that suggest changes to the proposed IEP will not be implemented unless the IEP is amended.

_____

_____

_____

GLOSSARY

Accommodations.   Techniques and materials that allow individuals with learning disabilities to complete school or work tasks with greater ease and effectiveness. Examples include spell-checkers, tape recorders, and expanded time for completing assignments.

Assistive technology.   Equipment that enhances the ability of students and employees to be more efficient and successful. For individuals with learning disabilities, computer grammar checkers, an overhead projector used by a teacher, or the audiovisual information delivered through a CD-ROM would be typical examples.

Attention Deficit Disorder (ADD).   A severe difficulty in focusing and maintaining attention. Often leads to learning and behavior problems at home, school, and work. Also called Attention Deficit Hyperactivity Disorder (ADHD).

Auditorily distractible.   Means paying attention to all sounds, not just the appropriate ones; for example, voices in hallways, the ringing of the telephone.

Brain imaging techniques.   Recently developed, noninvasive techniques for studying the activity of living brains. Includes brain electrical activity mapping (BEAM), computerized axial tomography (CAT), and magnetic resonance imaging (MRI).

Brain injury. The physical damage to brain tissue or structure that occurs before, during, or after birth that is verified by EEG, MRI, CAT, or a similar examination, rather than by observation of performance. When caused by an accident, the damage may be called Traumatic Brain Injury (TBI).

Collaboration. A program model in which the learning disabilities teacher demonstrates for or team-teaches with the general classroom teacher to help a student with learning disabilities be successful in a regular classroom.

Developmental aphasia. A severe language disorder that is presumed to be due to brain injury rather than a developmental delay in the normal acquisition of language.

Direct instruction. An instructional approach to academic subjects that emphasizes the use of carefully sequenced steps that include demonstration, modeling, guided practice, and independent application.

Distractibility. The child has difficulty blocking out unnecessary input from the environment.

Dyscalculia. A severe difficulty in understanding and using symbols or functions needed for success in mathematics.

Dysgraphia. A severe difficulty in producing handwriting that is legible and written at an age-appropriate speed.

Dyslexia. A severe difficulty in understanding or using one or more areas of language, including listening, speaking, reading, writing, and spelling.

Dysnomia. A marked difficulty in remembering names or recalling words needed for oral or written language.

Dyspraxia. A severe difficulty in performing drawing, writing, buttoning, and other tasks requiring fine motor skills, or in sequencing the necessary movements.

Hyperactivity. The child exhibits an unusual degree of activity. Most are fidgety; something is always in motion—fingers, pencil, or feet. They squirm in their seat, or cannot remain seated, and so forth.

Impulsivity.   The child does not think before acting or talking and does not consider the impact of his or her actions on others. Thus, the child does not learn from experience. This child may be accident-prone because of impulsive behavior combined with poor judgment.

Learned helplessness.   A tendency to be a passive learner who depends on others for decisions and guidance. In individuals with learning disabilities, continued struggle and failure can heighten this lack of self-confidence.

Learning modalities.   Approaches to assessment or instruction stressing the auditory, visual, or tactile avenues for learning that are dependent upon the individual.

Learning strategy approaches.   Instructional approaches that focus on efficient ways to learn, rather than on curriculum. Includes specific techniques for organizing, actively interacting with material, memorizing, and monitoring any content or subject.

Learning styles.   Approaches to assessment or instruction emphasizing the variations in temperament, attitude, and preferred manner of tackling a task. Typically considered are styles along the active/passive, reflective/impulsive, or verbal/spatial dimensions.

Locus of control.   The tendency to attribute success and difficulties either to internal factors such as effort or to external factors such as chance. Individuals with learning disabilities tend to blame failure on themselves and achievement on luck, leading to frustration and passivity.

Metacognitive learning.   Instructional approaches emphasizing the awareness of the cognitive processes that facilitate one's own learning and its application to academic and work assignments. Typical metacognitive techniques include systematic rehearsal of steps or conscious selection among strategies for completing a task.

Minimal Brain Dysfunction (MBD).   A medical and psychological term originally used to refer to the learning difficulties that seemed to result from identified or presumed damage to the brain. Reflects a medical, rather than educational or vocational, orientation.

Multisensory learning.   An instructional approach that combines auditory, visual, and tactile elements into a learning task. Tracing sandpaper numbers while saying a number fact aloud would be a multisensory learning activity.

Neuropsychological examination.   A series of tasks that allow observation of performance that is presumed to be related to the intactness of brain function.

Perceptual handicap.   Difficulty in accurately processing, organizing, and discriminating among visual, auditory, or tactile information. A person with a perceptual handicap may say that "cap/cup" sound the same or that "b" and "d" look the same. However, glasses or hearing aids do not necessarily indicate a perceptual handicap.

Prereferral process.   A procedure in which special and regular teachers develop trial strategies to help a student showing difficulty in learning remain in the regular classroom.

Resource program.   A program model in which a student with learning disabilities is in a regular classroom for most of each day, but also receives regularly scheduled individual services in a specialized learning-disabilities resource classroom.

Self-advocacy.   The development of specific skills and understandings that enable children and adults to explain their specific learning disabilities to others and cope positively with the attitudes of peers, parents, teachers, and employers.

Specific Language Disability (SLD).   A severe difficulty in some aspect of listening, speaking, reading, writing, or spelling, while skills in the other areas are age-appropriate. Also called Specific Language Learning Disability (SLLD).

Specific Learning Disability (SLD).   The official term used in federal legislation to refer to difficulty in certain areas of learning, rather than in all areas of learning. Synonymous with learning disabilities.

Subtype research.   A recently developed research method that seeks to identify characteristics that are common to specific groups within the larger population of individuals identified as having learning disabilities.

Transition.   Commonly used to refer to the change from secondary school to postsecondary programs, work, and independent living typical of young adults. Also used to describe other periods of major change such as from early childhood to school or from more specialized to mainstreamed settings.

Visually distractible.   Paying attention to everything visible rather than the appropriate items, for example, clouds, rug, pictures.

DISABILITY CHECKLISTS BY AGE

The following checklists describe activities, skills, or characteristics that professionals look for when determining if your child is developing at the proper pace. These are not inclusive, but can give you an idea of whether your child is developing too slowly for his age level, which can help you list your observations for your family doctor or your child's teacher. It is important not to panic if your child doesn't match her age's list exactly because it is normal for there to be a year or two difference in the pace of a young child's development.

Age Three Checklists

Table A.E.1. Physical Development Checklist

When we talk about physical development, we are talking about developing skills such as:			
Gross Motor		**Fine Motor**	
Children use large groups of muscles to sit, stand, walk, run, and so on, keeping balance and changing positions.	**Checklist** __Climbs well __Walks up and down stairs, alternating feet (one foot per stair step) __Kicks ball __Runs easily __Pedals tricycle __Bends over easily without falling	Three-year-olds are using their hands to eat, draw, dress, play, write, and do many other things.	**Checklist** __Makes up-and-down, side-to-side, and circular lines with pencil or crayon __Turns book pages one at a time __Builds a tower of more than six blocks __Holds a pencil in writing position __Screws and unscrews jar lids, nuts, and bolts __Turns rotating handles

Table A.E.2.   Social/Emotional Disabilities Checklist

Social		Emotional	
Social and emotional development is important because delays in development indicate not only possible emotional problems but also could indicate problems in areas such as cognition.			
When we talk about social/emotional development, we are talking about developing skills such as interacting with others; having relationships with family, friends, and teachers; cooperating; and responding to the feelings of others.	**Checklist** __Imitates adults and playmates __Spontaneously shows affection for familiar playmates __Can take turns in games (most of the time) __Understands concept of "mine" and "his/hers"	They develop social relationships with their playmates or peers and are able to express emotions of happiness, sadness, anger, frustration, and empathy. Preschoolers begin to be more comfortable separating from their parents.	**Checklist** __Expresses affection openly __Expresses a wide range of emotions __Separates easier from parents __Objects to major changes in routine

Table A.E.3.   Learning/Cognitive Disabilities Checklist

Cognitive		Language	
When we talk about cognitive and language development, we are talking about such things as:			
When we talk about learning or cognitive development, we are talking about developing skills such as thinking, learning, understanding, problem solving, reasoning, and remembering.	**Checklist** __Makes mechanical toys work __Plays make-believe with dolls, animals, and people __Sorts objects by shape and color __Completes puzzles with three or four pieces __Understands concept of "two" __Recognizes and identifies almost all common objects and pictures	When we talk about communication/language development, we are talking about developing skills such as speaking, using body language and gestures, communicating, and understanding what others say.	**Checklist** __Follows a two- or three-part command __Understands most sentences __Understands placement in space ("on," "in," "under") __Uses four- to five-word sentences __Can say name, age, and sex __Uses pronouns (I, you, me, we, they) and some plurals (cars, dogs, cats) __Matches an object in her hand or room to a picture in a book __Strangers can understand most of her words

Table A.E.4. Developmental Indicators Checklist

Developmental indicators are yardsticks of normal development; developmental delays indicate a problem of some kind.			
Developmental Indicators		**Developmental Delays**	
Developmental indicators give you an approximate yardstick by which you can monitor your child's progress.	**Checklist** __Walks with an agile, almost adult style __ Runs around obstacles __ Catches large balls and throws them overhead __ Climbs ladders and stairs __ Uses the slide __ Independently rides a tricycle __ Alternates feet when climbing __ Understands most of what is said __ 75 percent of speech is understandable __Speaks in complete sentences of three to five words __Matches pictures to objects __Learns by doing and through the senses __Understands concepts of "now," "soon," and "later" __ Begins to recognize cause-and-effect relationships __ Follows simple directions __ Enjoys helping with household tasks __ Begins to recognize own limits—asks for help __Likes to play alone, but near other children __Able to make choices between two things __Begins to notice other people's moods and feelings	Delays in development can indicate a need to formally diagnose conditions with associated developmental delays (e.g., Down syndrome, autism), and sensory impairments.	**Checklist** __Frequent falling and difficulty with stairs __Persistent drooling or very unclear speech __Cannot build a tower of more than four blocks __Difficulty manipulating small objects __ Cannot copy a circle by age three __Cannot communicate in short phrases __No involvement in "pretend" play __Does not understand simple instructions __Little interest in other children __ Extreme difficulty separating from mother or primary caregiver __Poor eye contact __ Limited interest in toys __Experiences a dramatic loss of skills he or she once had

Age Four Checklists

Table A.E.5.   Physical Development

When we talk about physical development, we are talking about developing such skills as:			
Gross Motor		**Fine Motor**	
Children should be using large groups of muscles to sit, stand, walk, run, change positions, and keep balance.	**Checklist** __Hops and stands on one foot up to five seconds __Goes upstairs and downstairs without support __Kicks ball forward __ Throws ball overhand __ Catches bounced ball most of the time __ Moves forward and backward with agility	Four-year-olds are using their hands to be able to eat, draw, dress, play, write, and do many other things.	**Checklist** __Copies square shapes __Draws a person with two to four body parts __Uses scissors __Draws circles and squares __Begins to copy some capital letters

Table A.E.6.   Social/Emotional Disabilities Checklist

Social and emotional development is important because delays in development indicate not only possible emotional problems but also could indicate problems in areas such as cognition.			
Social		**Emotional**	
When we talk about social/emotional development, we are talking about developing skills such as interacting with others; having relationships with family, friends, and teachers; cooperating; and responding to the feelings of others.	**Checklist** __Interested in new experiences __Cooperates with other children __ Plays "Mom" or "Dad" __Increasingly inventive in fantasy play __Dresses and undresses __Negotiates solutions to conflicts __More independent	Four-year-olds develop social relationships with their playmates or peers and are able to express the emotions of happiness, sadness, anger, frustration, and empathy.	**Checklist** __Imagines that many unfamiliar images may be "monsters" __Views self as a whole person involving body, mind, and feelings __Often cannot tell the difference between fantasy and reality

Table A.E.7. Learning/Cognitive Disabilities Checklist

When we talk about cognitive and language development, we are talking about things such as:			
Cognitive		**Language**	
When we talk about communication/language development, we are talking about developing skills such as speaking, using body language and gestures, communicating, and understanding what others say.	**Checklist** __Correctly names some colors __ Understands the concept of counting and may know a few numbers __ Tries to solve problems from a single point of view __ Begins to have a clearer sense of time __Follows three-part commands __Recalls parts of a story __Understands the concepts of "same" and "different" __Engages in fantasy play	By age four, a child can tell you her thoughts and experiences in addition to her everyday needs and wants. A four-year-old can ask questions about what happens around her. Every sound may not be produced clearly, but most people (not just a parent) can understand what she is saying.	**Checklist** __Has mastered some basic rules of grammar __Speaks in sentences of five to six words __Speaks clearly enough for strangers to understand __Tells stories

Table A.E.8. Developmental Checklist

Developmental indicators are yardsticks of normal development; developmental delays indicate a problem of some kind.			
Developmental Indicators		**Developmental Delays**	
Developmental indicators give you an approximate yardstick by which you can monitor your child's progress.	**Checklist** __Speaks fairly complex sentences ("The baby ate the cookie before I put it on the table") __Enjoys singing simple songs, rhymes, and nonsense words __Learns name and phone number, and if taught, may be able to print it	Delays in development can indicate a need to formally diagnose conditions with associated developmental delays (e.g., Down syndrome, autism), and sensory impairments.	**Checklist** __Cannot throw a ball overhand __Cannot jump in place __Cannot ride a tricycle __Cannot grasp a crayon between thumb and fingers

(continued)

Table A.E.8.   Developmental Checklist *(continued)*

Developmental Indicators		Developmental Delays	
	Checklist		**Checklist**
	__Follows two unrelated directions: "Put your milk on the table and get your coat on"		__Has difficulty scribbling
	__Uses a spoon, fork, and dinner knife skillfully		__Cannot stack four blocks
	__Dresses himself or herself without much help		__Still clings or cries whenever parents leave
	__Walks a straight line		__Shows no interest in interactive games
	__Hops on one foot		__Ignores other children
	__Pedals and steers a tricycle skillfully		__Doesn't respond to people outside the family
	__Jumps over objects five to six inches in height		
	__Places objects in a line from largest to smallest		__Doesn't engage in fantasy play
	__Recognizes some letters of the alphabet, if taught		__Resists dressing, sleeping, and using the toilet
	__Recognizes familiar words in simple books or signs (such as a Stop sign)		__Lashes out without any self-control when angry or upset
	__Counts one to seven objects out loud		__Cannot copy a circle
	__Understands and obeys simple rules (most of the time)		__Doesn't use sentences of more than three words
	__Takes turns and shares (most of the time), but may still be bossy		__Doesn't use "me" and "you" correctly
	__Changes the rules of a game as he or she goes along		__Experiences a dramatic loss of skills he or she once had
	__Has difficulty separating make believe from reality		

Age Five Checklists

Table A.E.9.   Physical Development

When we talk about physical development, we are talking about developing skills like:			
Gross Motor		**Fine Motor**	
Five-year-olds are using large groups of muscles more skillfully every day.	**Checklist** __Stands on one foot for ten seconds or longer __Hops __Can do somersaults __Swings __Climbs __May be able to skip	Five-year-olds use their hands to be able to eat, draw, dress, play, write, and do many other things.	**Checklist** __Copies triangle and other shapes __Draws a person with a body __Prints some letters __Dresses and undresses without help __Uses fork, spoon, and (sometimes) a table knife __Usually cares for own toilet needs

Table A.E.10.   Social/Emotional Disabilities Checklist

Social and emotional development is important because delays in development indicate not only possible emotional problems but also could indicate problems in areas such as cognition.			
Social		**Emotional**	
When we talk about social/emotional development, we are talking about developing skills such as interacting with others; having relationships with family, friends, and teachers; cooperating; and responding to the feelings of others.	**Checklist** __Wants to please friends __Wants to be like her friends __More likely to agree to rules __Likes to sing, dance, and act __Shows more independence and may even visit a next-door neighbor by herself	They develop social relationships with their playmates or peers and are able to express emotions of happiness, sadness, anger, frustration, and empathy.	**Checklist** __Aware of gender __Able to distinguish fantasy from reality __Sometimes demanding, sometimes eagerly cooperative

Table A.E.11. Learning/Cognitive Disabilities Checklists

When we talk about cognitive and language development, we are talking about such things as:			
Cognitive		**Language**	
When we talk about communication/language development, we are talking about developing skills such as speaking, using body language and gestures, communicating, and understanding what others say.	**Checklist** __Can count ten or more objects __Correctly names at least four colors __Better understands the concept of time __Knows about things used every day in the home (money, food, and appliances)	A five-year-old is beginning to acquire complex thinking. He can comment on his environment and answer questions that involve thinking creatively about what usually happens, might happen, and has happened. He knows who he is and what his relationship is to the people around him. A five-year-old child can have a reasonable, intelligible conversation with his family and peers about activities that relate to his daily life. A five-year-old is beginning to have intelligible and more complex conversations with his family, teachers, and friends. He can tell you about relationships and how those relationships pertain to him. His thought processes are becoming more developed, so he is beginning to communicate thoughts and ideas that involve thinking creatively such as predictions or time concepts.	**Checklist** __Recalls part of a story __Speaks sentences of more than five words __Uses future tense __Tells longer stories __Says name and address

Table A.E.12. Developmental Checklists

Developmental indicators are yardsticks of normal development; developmental delays indicate a problem of some kind.			
Developmental indicators		**Developmental Delays**	
Developmental indicators give you an approximate yardstick by which you can monitor your child's progress.	**Checklist** __Verbally communicates needs, wants, and thoughts __Uses complete sentences to recount an event __Asks questions	Delays in development can indicate a need to formally diagnose conditions with associated developmental delays (e.g., Down syndrome, autism), and sensory impairments.	**Checklist** __Acts extremely fearful or timid __Acts extremely aggressive __Is unable to separate from parents without major protest __Is easily distracted and unable to concentrate on any single activity for more than five minutes

Table A.E.12. Developmental Checklists *(continued)*

Developmental Indicators		Developmental Delays	
	Checklist		**Checklist**
	__Goes to the bathroom by herself		__Shows little interest in playing with other children
	__Can wash and dry hands		__Refuses to respond to people in general, or responds only superficially
	__Can put on and button or zip own coat		__Rarely uses fantasy or imitation in play
	__Shares and takes turns when playing with other children		__Seems unhappy or sad much of the time
	__Can easily separate from parents		__Doesn't engage in a variety of activities
	__Approaches new activities with enthusiasm and curiosity		__Avoids or seems aloof with other children and adults
	__Follows two-step directions		__Doesn't express a wide range of emotions
	__Runs, hops, walks, skips, and throws a ball.		__Has trouble eating, sleeping, or using the toilet
	__Holds crayons, pencils, and scissors properly		__Can't tell the difference between fantasy and reality
			__Seems unusually passive
			__Cannot understand two-part commands using prepositions ("Put the doll on the bed, and get the ball under the couch.")
			__Can't correctly give her first and last name
			__Doesn't use plurals or past tense properly when speaking
			__Doesn't talk about her daily activities and experiences
			__Cannot build a tower of six to eight blocks
			__Seems uncomfortable holding a crayon
			__Has trouble taking off clothing
			__Cannot brush her teeth efficiently
			__Cannot wash and dry her hands
			__Experiences a dramatic loss of skills he or she once had

Age Six Checklists

Table A.E.13.   Physical Development

In the early school years, you won't see dramatic changes in motor skills because this is a period of refinement, when coordination improves and fine motor skills are sharpened.

Gross Motor Development		Fine Motor Development	
A six-year-old will be gaining more control of large muscle groups and is able to try new activities.	**Checklist** __May still be somewhat uncoordinated and gawky __Able to learn to ride a bicycle __Can move in time with music or a beat	Fine motor skills continue to develop rapidly at this age, and you should be seeing your child successfully attempt increasingly discreet movements.	**Checklist** __Holds a pencil __Uses scissors __Uses a keyboard with one finger __Operates a mouse __Operates video game features

Table A.E.14.   Social/Emotional Disabilities Checklist

Your child will experience many emotional and social changes over the coming years. Here are some of them:

Emotional Development		Social Development	
Six-year-olds are becoming less egocentric, but it is a difficult transition. You should see your child trying to become more inclusive of others' feelings, but also struggling with placement of his or her own feelings.	**Checklist** __May be hurt by criticism, blame, or punishment __Can be rigid, demanding, and unable to adapt __Increasingly aware that others have may have different feelings __Becomes competitive	Normal six-year-old development involves establishing independent friendships and activities. Children may have an increased need for adult approval to feel comfortable with their attempts at autonomy.	**Checklist** __Exchanges best friends and enemies easily __Grows more independent, yet feels less secure __Craves affection from parents and teachers __Friendships are unstable; can be unkind to peers, needs to win, and may change rules to suit herself __Exhibits bossy behavior __Seeks adult and peer approval __Maintains important friendships outside of the classroom __Becomes interested in the opposite sex __Is competitive __Wants to choose work partners __Sees adult inconsistencies and imperfections

Table A.E.15.   Learning/Cognitive Disabilities Checklist

Your child should be achieving many learning milestones such as:			
Cognitive		**Language**	
Six-year-olds are able to think in more complex ways.	**Checklist** __Moving toward abstract thinking __Develops reasoning skills __Wants it all; has difficulty making choices	Six-year-olds are increasing language development rapidly.	**Checklist** __Uses a vocabulary of 1,000 words or so. __Shifts from learning through observation and experience to learning via language and logic __Understands that letters represent the sounds that form words __Forms complex sentences; writes simple sentences __Attempts to use punctuation __Writes one-sentence paragraphs

Table A.E.16.   Developmental Checklist

Developmental indicators are yardsticks of normal development; developmental delays indicate a problem of some kind.			
Developmental Indicators		**Developmental Delays**	
Developmental indicators give you an approximate yardstick by which you can monitor your child's progress.	**Checklist** __Follows two-step oral directions __Listens attentively for ten minutes or more __Draws a picture of their whole self (not just a head, but a head with a neck and torso, and so on)	Delays in development can indicate a need to formally diagnose conditions with associated developmental delays (e.g., Down syndrome, autism) and sensory impairments.	**Checklist** __Is unable to follow simple directions __Includes odd details and excludes other details in self-portraits __Is unable to listen attentively

(continued)

Table A.E.16. Developmental Checklist *(continued)*

Developmental Indicators		Developmental Delays	
	Checklist		**Checklist**
	__Tells exactly how old they are and how old they will be next year ("I am six-and-a-half years old; I'll be seven.")		__Doesn't understand that doing something can cause something else to happen (cause and effect)
	__Thinks logically some of the time		__Doesn't follow rules well
	__Reasons		__Can't remember colors, numbers, or letters
	__Understands concept of cause and effect		__Fine motor skills are developing at a slower pace than others
	__Learns well through active involvement		__Doesn't understand basic reasoning
	__Continues to develop fine motor skills		__Mumbles, slurs, or has trouble pronouncing words
	__Plays board and card games		__Is a concrete thinker
	__Follows the rules		
	__Names colors		
	__Knows his or her phone number and address		
	__Speaks clearly		
	__States things as negatives: "I hate it," "I can't," "boooring," "yeah, right"		
	__Embraces abstract thoughts		

Age Seven Checklists

Table A.E.17. Physical Development

In the early school years, you won't see dramatic changes in motor skills because this is a period of refinement, when coordination improves and fine motor skills are sharpened.			
Gross Motor Development		**Fine Motor Development**	
Large muscle group development is becoming easier and easier.	**Checklist** __Hand-eye coordination is well developed __Has good balance __Can execute simple gymnastic movements, such as somersaults __Catches small balls	Your child should have very skilled fine motor movements.	**Checklist** __Uses scissors to cut fine details __Draws more finely detailed drawings __Handwriting improves __Writes smaller letters __Keyboarding skills increase __Performs intricate video game features __Ties shoelaces

Table A.E.18. Social/Emotional Disabilities Checklists

Social and emotional development is important because delays in development indicate not only possible emotional problems but also could indicate problems in areas such as cognition.			
Emotional Development		**Social Development**	
When we talk about social/emotional development, we are talking about developing skills such as interacting with others; having relationships with family, friends, and teachers; cooperating; and responding to the feelings of others.	**Checklist** __Worries more __May have low self-confidence __Tends to complain __Has strong emotional reactions __Understands the difference between right and wrong __Starts to feel guilt and shame __Views life in absolutes		**Checklist** __Desires to be perfect and is quite self-critical __Takes direction well; needs punishment only rarely __Avoids and withdraws from adults __Is a better loser and less likely to place blame __Waits for her turn in activities __Wants to spend a lot of time with friends __Enjoys rules, rituals, and routines __Enjoys younger children __Begins to understand others' views

Table A.E.19. Learning/Cognitive Disabilities Checklists:

Your child should be achieving many learning milestones such as:			
Cognitive		**Language**	
When we talk about communication/ language development, we are talking about developing skills such as speaking, using body language and gestures, communicating, and understanding what others say.	**Checklist** __Demonstrates a longer attention span __Uses serious, logical thinking __Is thoughtful and reflective __Able to understand reasoning and make the right decisions __Can tell time; knows the days, months, and seasons __Describes points of similarity between two objects __Able to solve more complex problems __Individual learning style becomes more clear-cut __Begins to understand others' views	Language skills should be developing rapidly.	**Checklist** __Uses a vocabulary of several thousand words __Writes two-sentence paragraphs __Uses simple punctuation

Table A.E.20. Developmental Checklists

Developmental indicators are yardsticks of normal development; developmental delays indicate a problem of some kind.			
Developmental Indicators		**Developmental Delays**	
Developmental indicators give you an approximate yardstick by which you can monitor your child's progress.	**Checklist** __Enjoys testing his or her own strength and skills __Prints full name __Reverses letters ("b" becomes a "d") __Plans and builds objects (crafts) __Reads often __Identifies the difference between left and right __Knows days of the week __Is interested in doing things correctly __Doesn't like to have accomplishments ignored	Delays in development can indicate a need to formally diagnose conditions with associated developmental delays (e.g., Down syndrome, autism) and sensory impairments.	**Checklist** __Isn't physical __Isn't writing __Is not interested in reading __Doesn't know left from right __Is unaware of most time—seasons, months, days

Age Eight Checklists

Table A.E.21.   Physical Development

In the early school years, you won't see dramatic changes in motor skills because this is a period of refinement, when coordination improves and fine motor skills are sharpened.			
Gross Motor Development		**Fine Motor Development**	
Large muscle groups are gaining strength, and your child's stamina should be increasing.	**Checklist** __Stamina increases; can run and swim further __Enjoys testing his or her own strength and skills __Has good balance __Able to catch smaller balls	Your child should have very skilled fine motor movements.	**Checklist** __Finger control is quite refined __Manipulates small tools well __Ties shoelaces

Table A.E.22.   Social/Emotional Disabilities Checklist

Social and emotional development is important because delays in development indicate not only possible emotional problems but also could indicate problems in areas such as cognition.			
Emotional Development		**Social Development**	
When we talk about social/emotional development, we are talking about developing skills such as interacting with others; having relationships with family, friends, and teachers; cooperating; and responding to the feelings of others.	**Checklist** __Has strong need for love and understanding, especially from mother __Can be helpful, cheerful, and pleasant as well as rude, bossy, and selfish __May be quite sensitive and overly dramatic __Emotions change quickly __Impatient; finds waiting for special events torturous __Can be obsessed with, and motivated by, money __Enjoys rules, rituals, and routines	Socially your child should be developing rapidly.	**Checklist** __Favors group play, clubs, and team sports; wants to feel part of a group __More influenced by peer pressure __Chooses the same gender friends more often than not __Understands others' views (but still is focused primarily on self) __Enjoys younger children __Wants to be with friends often

Table A.E.23. Learning/Cognitive Disabilities Checklist

Your child should be achieving many learning milestones such as:			
Cognitive		**Language**	
When we talk about communication/ language development, we are talking about developing skills such as speaking, using body language and gestures, communicating, and understanding what others say.	**Checklist** __Seeks to understand the reasons for things __Begins to feel competent in skills and have preferences for some activities and subjects __Thinking is organized and logical __Begins to recognize concept of reversibility ($4 + 2 = 6$ and $6 - 2 = 4$)	Language skills are becoming more and more sophisticated.	**Checklist** __Can converse at an almost-adult level __Reading may be a major interest

Table A.E.24. Developmental Checklist

Developmental indicators are yardsticks of normal development; developmental delays indicate a problem of some kind.			
Developmental Indicators		**Developmental Delays**	
Developmental indicators give you an approximate yardstick by which you can monitor your child's progress.	**Checklist** __Prints his or her own name __Enjoys planning and building activities __Reads often __Identifies the difference between left and right __Recites the days of the week __Wants to do things correctly	Delays in development can indicate a need to formally diagnose conditions with associated developmental delays (e.g., Down syndrome, autism) and sensory impairments.	**Checklist** __Is unable to print first name __Can't tell left from right __Doesn't plan __Doesn't know days or weeks

INTERNET RESOURCES

State	State Web Site	State Forms and Publications
Alabama	http://www.alsde.edu/ html/sections/section_detail .asp?section=65&footer=sections	http://www.alsde.edu/html/sections/ documents.asp?section=65&sort=7&footer= sections
Alaska	http://www.educ.state.ak.us/tls/SPED/ home.html	
Arizona	http://www.ade.state.az.us/ess/ ESSHome.asp	http://www.ade.state.az.us/ess/forms.asp
Arkansas	http://arksped.k12.ar.us/	
California	http://www.cde.ca.gov/sp/se/	
Colorado	http://www.cde.state.co.us/cdesped/ index.asp	
Connecticut	http://www.state.ct.us/sde/deps/	http://www.state.ct.us/sde/deps/special/ index.htm#IEP
Delaware	http://www.doe.state. de.us/programs/specialed/	http://www.doe.k12.de.us/exceptional_child/ forms.htm
District of Columbia	http://www.k12.dc.us/dcps/specialed/ dcpsspecedhome.html	

(continued)

(continued)

State	State Web Site	State Forms and Publications
Florida	http://www.firn.edu/doe/commhome/index.html	http://www.firn.edu/doe/commhome/pub-home.htm
Georgia	http://public.doe.k12.ga.us/ci_excep tional.aspx	http://public.doe.k12.ga.us/ci_exceptional.aspx?PageReq=CIEXCForms
Hawaii	http://doe.k12.hi.us/specialeducation/index.htm	http://doe.k12.hi.us/specialeducation/index_references.htm
Idaho	http://www.sde.state.id.us/SpecialEd/	
Illinois	http://www.isbe.state.il.us/spec-ed/default.htm	http://www.isbe.state.il.us/spec-ed/html/forms.htm
Indiana	http://doe.state.in.us/exceptional/speced/welcome.html	
Iowa	http://www.iowaccess.org/educate/ecese/cfcs/speced/index.html	
Kansas	http://www.kansped.org/	http://www.kansped.org/ksde/laws/legal reqmts.html
Kentucky	http://www.education.ky.gov/NR/exeres/2A3316FF-32DF-46DD-8BD2–5D27DADD239D.htm	http://www.education.ky.gov/KDE/Instructional+Resources/Student+and+Family+Support/Exceptional+Children/Forms+and+Documents/default.htm
Louisiana	http://www.doe.state.la.us/lde/specialp/home.html	http://www.doe.state.la.us/lde/specialp/505.html
Maine	http://www.maine.gov/education/speced/index.htm	http://www.maine.gov/education/speced/forms.htm
Maryland	http://www.marylandpublicschools.org/MSDE/divisions/earlyinterv/	
Massachusetts	http://www.doe.mass.edu/sped/	http://www.doe.mass.edu/sped/iep/
Michigan	http://www.michigan.gov/mde/0,1607,7–140–6530_6598–-,00.html	http://www.michigan.gov/mde/0,1607,7–140–6530_6598_36168–-,00.html
Minnesota	http://education.state.mn.us/mde/Learning_Support/Special_Education/index.html	

State	State Web Site	State Forms and Publications
Mississippi	http://www.mde.k12.ms.us/special_education/	http://www.mde.k12.ms.us/special_educa tion/just_for_parents.html
Missouri	http://dese.mo.gov/divspeced/	http://dese.mo.gov/divspeced/Publications/index.html
Montana	http://www.opi.mt.gov/SpecEd/index.html	http://www.opi.mt.gov/SpecEd/Forms.html
Nebraska	http://www.nde.state.ne.us/SPED/sped.html	http://www.nde.state.ne.us/SPED/forms/srformshp.html
Nevada	http://www.doe.nv.gov/edteam/ndeoffices/sped-diversity-improve.html	http://www.doe.nv.gov/edteam/ndeoffices/sped-diversity-improve/docs.html
New Hampshire	http://www.ed.state.nh.us/education/doe/organization/instruction/bose.htm	http://www.ed.state.nh.us/education/doe/organization/instruction/SpecialEd/Forms.htm
New Jersey	http://www.nj.gov/njded/specialed/	http://www.nj.gov/njded/specialed/form/
New Mexico	http://www.ped.state.nm.us/seo/index.htm	http://www.ped.state.nm.us/seo/parents/index.htm
New York	http://www.vesid.nysed.gov/specialed/	http://www.vesid.nysed.gov/specialed/applications/home.html
North Carolina	http://www.dpi.state.nc.us/ec/	http://www.dpi.state.nc.us/ec/policy/forms/
North Dakota	http://www.dpi.state.nd.us/speced/index.shtm	http://www.dpi.state.nd.us/speced/forms/index.shtm
Ohio	http://www.ode.state.oh.us/exceptional_children/	http://www.ode.state.oh.us/exceptional_children/Children_with_Disabilities/default.asp
Oklahoma	http://sde.state.ok.us/home/defaultie.html	http://www.sde.state.ok.us/pro/spedpp.html
Oregon	http://www.ode.state.or.us/search/results/?id=40	http://www.ode.state.or.us/pubs/sped/
Pennsylvania	http://www.pde.state.pa.us/special_edu/site/default.asp?g=0&special_eduNav=|978|	http://www.pde.state.pa.us/special_edu/cwp/view.asp?a=3&q=113158

(continued)

(continued)

State	State Web Site	State Forms and Publications
Rhode Island	http://www.ridoe.net/Special_needs/Default.htm	
South Carolina	http://www.myscschools.com/offices/ec/	http://www.myscschools.com/offices/ec/page1396.cfm
Tennessee	http://www.state.tn.us/education/speced/	http://www.state.tn.us/education/speced/seforms.php
Texas	http://www.tea.state.tx.us/special.ed/	http://www.tea.state.tx.us/special.ed/forrns/
Utah	http://www.schools.utah.gov/sars/	
Vermont	http://www.state.vt.us/educ/new/html/pgm_sped.html	http://www.state.vt.us/educ/new/html/pgm_sped/forms.html
Virginia	http://www.pen.k12.va.us/VDOE/sess/	http://www.pen.k12.va.us/VDOE/Forms/
Washington	http://www.k12.wa.us/SpecialEd/default.aspx	http://www.k12.wa.us/SpecialEd/forms.aspx
West Virginia	http://wvde.state.wv.us/ose/	
Wisconsin	http://www.dpi.state.wi.us/sped/tm-specedtopics.html	http://www.dpi.state.wi.us/sped/form_int.html
Wyoming	http://www.k12.wy.us/sp.asp	http://www.k12.wy.us/ep/sp/programs/speced/forms.asp

Organization	Web Site
American Printing House for the Blind	http://www.aph.org/
Council for Exceptional Children	http://www.cec.sped.org/
National Center for Learning Disabilities	http://www.ncld.org/
National Dissemination Center for Children with Disabilities	http://www.nichcy.org/
Special-education acronyms	http://www.educ.state.ak.us/tls/SPED/Acronyms.html
Office of Special Education Programs (OSEP)	http://www.ed.gov/about/offices/list/osers/osep/index.html
National Information Clearinghouse on Children Who Are Deaf-Blind	http://www.tr.wou.edu/dblink/
Family Village	http://www.waisman.wisc.edu/kennedy/index.htmlx
Parent Advocacy Coalition for Educational Rights	http://www.pacer.org/
New Mexico Public Education Department list of disability Web sites	http://www.ped.state.nm.us/seo/links/atoz.htm
Dictionary of terms	http://www.usd.edu/cd/publications/dictionary.pdf
Learning Disabilities Association of America	www.ldanatl.org

REFERENCES

Adler, R. (1989). Library orientation: Intervention strategies for students with learning disabilities. *Journal of Postsecondary Education and Disability, 7*(2), 45–52.

Anderson, P. L. (1993). *Issues in assessment and diagnosis.* In L. C. Brinckerhoff, S. F. Shaw, and J. M. McGuire (eds.), *Promoting postsecondary education for students with learning disabilities* (pp. 89–136). Austin, Tex.: PRO-ED.

Aune, E. (1991). A transition model for post-secondary bound students with learning disabilities. *Learning Disabilities Research and Practice, 6,* 177–187.

Aune, E., and Ness, J. (1991). *Tools for transition: Preparing students with learning disabilities for postsecondary education.* Circle Pines, Minn.: American Guidance Service.

Bandura, A. (1986). *Social foundations of thought and action: A social cognitive theory.* Englewood Cliffs, N.J.: Prentice-Hall.

Bandura, A. (1997). *Self-efficacy: The exercise of control.* New York: Freeman.

Barr, V., Hartman, R., and Spillane, S. (1998). Getting ready for college: Advising high school students with learning disabilities. *The Postsecondary LD Report.*

Barton, J. M., and Starnes, W. T. (1989). Identifying distinguishing characteristics of gifted and talented/learning disabled students. *Roeper Review, 12,* 23–29.

Baum, S. (1984). Meeting the needs of the learning disabled gifted students. *Roeper Review, 7,* 16–19.

Baum, S. M., Renzulli, J. S., and Hebert, T. P. (1994). Reversing underachievement: Stories of success. *Educational Leadership, 52,* 48–53.

Biller, E. (1985). *Understanding and guiding the career development of adolescents and young adults with learning disabilities.* Springfield, Ill.: Thomas.

Borkowski, J. G., and Thorpe, P. K. (1994). Self-regulation and motivation: A life-span perspective. In D. H. Schunk and B. J. Zimmerman (eds.), *Self-regulation of learning and performance: Issues and educational implications* (pp. 45–74). Hillsdale, N.J.: Erlbaum.

Bouffard-Bouchard, T., Parent, S., and Larivee, S. (1993). Self-regulation on a concept-formation task among average and gifted students. *Journal of Experimental Child Psychology, 56,* 115–134.

Bragstad, B. J., and Stumpf, S. M. (1987). *A guidebook for teaching: Study skills and motivation* (2nd ed.). Newton, Mass.: Allyn & Bacon.

Brinckerhoff, L. C. (1994). Developing effective self-advocacy skills in college-bound students with learning disabilities. *Intervention in School and Clinic, 29,* 229–237.

Brinckerhoff, L. C., McGuire, J. M., and Shaw, S. F. (eds.). (2002). *Postsecondary education and transition for students with learning disabilities* (2nd ed.). Austin, Tex.: PRO-ED.

Brinckerhoff, L. C., Shaw, S. F., and McGuire, J. M. (eds.). (1993). *Promoting postsecondary education for students with learning disabilities: A handbook for practitioners.* Austin, Tex.: PRO-ED.

Bryant, B. R., Bryant, D. P., and Rieth, H. J. (2002). The use of assistive technology in postsecondary education. In L. C. Brinckerhoff, J. M. McGuire, and S. F. Shaw (eds.), *Postsecondary education and transition for students with learning disabilities* (2nd ed.) (pp. 389–430). Austin, Tex.: PRO-ED.

Bursuck, W. D., and Jayanthi, M. (1993). Strategy instruction: Programming for independent study skills usage. In S. A. Vogel and P. B. Adelman (eds.), *Success for college students with learning disabilities* (pp. 177–205). New York: Springer-Verlag.

Butler, D. L. (1998). A strategic content learning approach to promoting self-regulated learning by students with learning disabilities. In D. H. Schunk and B. J. Zimmerman (eds.), *Self-regulated learning: From teaching to self-reflective practice* (pp. 160–183). New York: Guilford Press.

Corno, L. (1989). Self-regulated learning: A volitional analysis. In B. J. Zimmerman and D. H Schunk (eds.), *Self-regulated learning and academic achievement: Theory, research, and practice* (pp. 111–141). New York: Springer-Verlag.

Corno, L., and Kanfer, R. (1993). The role of volition in learning and performance. In L. Darling-Hammond (ed.), *Review of research in education* (vol. 19, pp. 301–341). Washington, D.C.: American Educational Research Association.

Cowen, S. (1993). Transition planning for LD college-bound students. In S. A. Vogel and P. B. Adelman (eds.), *Success for college students with learning disabilities* (pp. 39–56). New York: Springer-Verlag.

Dalke, C. (1993). Programming for independent study skills usage. In S. S. Vogel and P. B. Adelman (eds.), *Success for college students with learning disabilities* (pp. 57–80). New York: Springer-Verlag.

Dalke, C., and Howard, D. (1994). *Life works: A transition program for high school students.* East Moline, Ill.: LinguiSystems.

Day, S. L., and Edwards, B. J. (1996). Assistive technology for postsecondary students with learning disabilities. *Journal of Learning Disabilities, 29,* 486–493.

Deci, E. L., and Ryan, R. M. (1985). *Intrinsic motivation and self-determinism in human motivation.* New York: Plenum Press.

Deshler, D. D., Ellis, E. S., and Lenz, B. K. (1996). *Teaching adolescents with learning disabilities: Strategies and methods* (2nd ed.). Denver: Love.

DuChossois, G., and Stein, E. (1992). *Choosing the right college: A step-by-step system to aid the students with learning disabilities in selecting the suitable college for them.* New York: New York University.

Eaton, H. (1996). *How students with learning disabilities can make the transition from high school to college.* Santa Barbara, Calif.: Excel Publishing.

Eaton, H., and Coull, L. (1998). *Transitions to postsecondary learning: Self-advocacy handbook.* Vancouver, B.C.: Eaton Coull Learning Group.

Ellis, E. S. (1990). What's so strategic about teaching teachers to teach strategies? *Teacher Education and Special Education, 13,* 56–62.

Field, S., and Hoffman, A. (1996). Increasing the ability of educators to support youth and self-determination. In L. E. Powers, G.H.S. Singer, and J. Sowers (eds.), *Promoting self-competence in children and youth with disabilities: On the road to autonomy* (pp. 171–187). Baltimore: Brookes.

Gardner, H. (1983). *Frames of mind: The theory of multiple intelligences.* New York: Basic Books.

Gardner, H. (1993). *Multiple intelligences: The theory in practice.* New York: Basic Books.

Gardner, H. (1999). *Intelligence reframed: Multiple intelligences for the 21st century.* New York: Basic Books.

Garner, R. (1990). When children and adults do not use learning strategies. *Review of Educational Research, 60,* 517–530.

Gerber, P. J., Ginsberg, R., and Reiff, H. B. (1992). Identifying alterable patterns in employment success for highly successful adults with learning disabilities. *Journal of Learning Disabilities, 25,* 475–487.

Gerber, P. J., and Reiff, H. B. (1991). *Speaking for themselves: Ethnographic interviews with adults with learning disabilities.* Ann Arbor: University of Michigan Press.

Henderson, C. (1999). *College freshmen with disabilities.* Washington, D.C.: American Council on Education, HEATH Resource Center.

Heyward, S. (1998). *Disability and higher education: Guidance for Section 504 and ADA compliance.* Horsham, Penn.: LRP Publications.

Higgins, E. L., and Raskind, M. H. (1995). An investigation of the compensatory effectiveness of speech recognition on the written composition performance of postsecondary students with learning disabilities. *Learning Disability Quarterly, 18,* 159–174.

Hodge, B. M., and Preston-Sabin, J. (1997) (eds.). *Accommodations—or just good teaching? Strategies for teaching college students with disabilities.* Westport, Conn.: Praeger.

Hoover, E. (2002, July 26). Removing the "scarlet letter." *The Chronicle of Higher Education,* pp. A41–42.

Individuals with Disabilities Education Act Amendments of 1997, 20 U.S.C. §1400 *et seq.*

Jarrow, J. E. (1997). *Higher education and the LDA: Issues and perspectives.* Columbus, Ohio: Disability Access Information and Support.

King, W., and Jarrow, J. (1990). *Testing accommodations for students with disabilities.* Columbus, Ohio: AHEAD.

Koehler, M., and Kravets, M. (1998). *Counseling secondary students with learning disabilities.* Paramas, N.J.: Prentice-Hall.

Krouse, J. H., and Krouse, H. J. (1981). Toward a multimodal theory of academic achievement. *Educational Psychologist, 16,* 151–164.

Kuhl, J. (1984). Volitional aspects of achievement motivation and learned helplessness: Toward a comprehensive theory of action control. In B. Maher and W. Maher (eds.), *Progress in experimental personality research* (vol. 13, pp. 99–171). New York: Academic Press.

Kuhl, J. (1992). A theory of self-regulation: Action versus state orientation, self-discrimination, and some applications. *Applied Psychology: An International Review, 41,* 97–129.

Latham, P. S., and Latham, P. H. (1998). Legal issues regarding AD/HD at the postsecondary level: Implications for service providers. In P. Quinn and A. McGormick (eds.), *Re-thinking AD/HD: A guide to fostering success in students with AD/HD at the college level* (pp. 102–107). Bethesda, Md.: Advantage Books.

Lewis, L., and Farris, E. (1999). *An institutional perspective on students with disabilities in postsecondary education* (NCES 1999–046). Washington, D.C.: U. S. Department of Education, Office of Educational Research and Improvement.

Maker, C. J. (1978). *The self-perceptions of successful handicapped scientists.* (Grant No. G00–7701[905]). Washington, D.C.: U.S. Department of Health, Education, and Welfare, Office of Education, Bureau of the Education for the Handicapped.

Mangrum, C. T., and Strichart, S. (1997). *Peterson's colleges with programs for students with learning disabilities or attention-deficit disorders.* Princeton, N.J.: Peterson's.

McGuire, J. M. (1998). Educational accommodations: A university administrator's view. In M. Gordon and S. Keiser (eds.), *Accommodations in higher education under the Americans with Disabilities Act (ADA)* (pp. 20–45). New York: Guilford Press.

McGuire, J. M., Hall, D., and Litt, A. V. (1991). A field-based study of the direct service needs of college students with learning disabilities. *Journal of College Student Development, 32*, 101–108.

McGuire, J. M., and Madaus, J. W. (1999). *The University of Connecticut Program for College Students with Learning Disabilities (UPLD): 1988–1999.* Storrs, Conn.: Postsecondary Education Disability Unit, Neag School of Education.

McGuire, J. M., and Shaw, S. F. (1987). A decision-making process for the college-bound student. Matching learner, institution, and support program. *Learning Disability Quarterly, 10*(2), 106–111.

McNaughton, D., Hughes, C., and Clark, K. (1993). *An investigation of the effect of five writing conditions on the spelling performance of college students with disabilities.* Paper presented at the 30th international conference of the Learning Disability Association of America, San Francisco.

Neihardt, M., Reis, S. M., Robinson, N., and Moon, S. M. (eds.). (2001). *The social and emotional development of gifted children. What do we know?* Waco, Tex.: Prufrock Press.

Nolen, S. B., and Flaladyna, T. M. (1990). Personal and environmental influences on students' beliefs about effective study strategies. *Contemporary Educational Psychology, 15*, 116–130.

Olenchak, F. R. (1994). Talent development: Accommodating the social and emotional needs of secondary gifted/learning-disabled students. *Journal of Secondary Gifted Education, 5*, 40–52.

Olenchak, F. R. (1995). Effects of enrichment on gifted/learning-disabled students. *Journal for the Education of the Gifted, 18*, 385–399.

Patton, J., and Dunn, C. (1998). *Transition from school to young adulthood.* Austin, Tex.: PRO-ED.

Patton, J. R., and Polloway, E. A. (eds.). (1996). *Learning disabilities: The challenges of adulthood.* Austin, Tex.: PRO-ED.

Perry, N. E. (2002). Introduction: Using qualitative methods to enrich understanding of self-regulated learning. *Educational Psychologist, 37*(1), 1–4.

Phipps, R., and Merisotis, S. J. (1999). *What's the difference? A review of contemporary research on the effectiveness of distance learning in higher education.* Washington, D.C.: Institute for Higher Education Policy. Accessed on September 4, 2007, from http://www.ihep.com/difference.pdf.

Pintrich, P. R. (1995). Understanding self-regulated learning. In R. J. Menges and M. D. Svinicki (eds.), *New directions for teaching and learning* (vol. 63, pp. 3–12). San Francisco: Jossey-Bass.

Pintrich, P. R., Anderman, E. M., and Klobukar, C. (1994). Intraindividual differences in motivation and cognition in students with and without learning disabilities. *Journal of Learning Disabilities, 27,* 360–370.

Pintrich, P. R., and De Groot, E. (1990). Motivational and self-regulated components of classroom academic performance. *Journal of Educational Psychology, 82,* 33–40.

Pintrich, P. R., and Garcia, T. (1991). Students' goal orientation and self-regulation in the college classroom. *Advances in Motivation and Achievement, 7,* 371–402.

Pintrich, P. R., and Schrauben, B. (1992). Students' motivational beliefs and their cognitive engagement in classroom tasks. In D. Schunk and J. Meece (eds.), *Student perceptions in the classroom: Causes and consequences* (pp. 149–183). Hillsdale, N.J.: Erlbaum.

Policastro, M. M. (1993). Assessing and developing metacognitive attributes in college students with learning disabilities. In S. A. Vogel and P. B. Adelman (eds.), *Success for college students with learning disabilities* (pp. 151–176). New York: Springer-Verlag.

Pressley, M., and McGormick, C. B. (1995). *Advanced educational psychology for educators, researchers, and policymakers.* New York: HarperCollins.

Price, L. (1988). Support groups work! *Journal of Counseling and Human Services Professions, 2,* 35–46.

Purcell, J. H., and Renzulli, J. S. (1998). *Total talent portfolio: A systematic plan to identify and nurture gifts and talents.* Mansfield, Conn.: Creative Learning Press.

Raskind, M., and Higgins, E. (1998). Assistive technology for postsecondary students with learning disabilities: An overview. *Journal of Learning Disabilities, 31*(1), 27–40.

Reis, S. M., McGuire, J. M., and Neu, T. W. (2000). Compensation strategies used by high ability students with learning disabilities. *Gifted Child Quarterly, 44*(2), 123–134.

Reis, S. M., Neu, T. W., and McGuire, J. M. (1995). *Talents in two places: Case studies of high ability students with learning disabilities who have achieved.* Research monograph no. 95114. Storrs, Conn.: National Research Center on the Gifted and Talented.

Renzulli, J. S. (1977). *The Enrichment Triad Model: A guide for developing defensible programs for the gifted and talented.* Mansfield Center, Conn.: Creative Learning Press.

Renzulli, J. S. (1978). What makes giftedness? *Phi Delta Kappan, 60*(3), 180–184, 261.

Renzulli, J. S. (1986). The three-ring conception of giftedness: A developmental model for creative productivity. In R. J. Sternberg and J. E. Davidson (eds.), *Conceptions of Giftedness* (pp. 53–92). New York: Cambridge University Press.

Renzulli, J. S., and Reis, S. M. (1991). The reform movement and the quiet crisis in gifted education. *Gifted Child Quarterly, 35*(1), 26–35.

Renzulli, J. S., and Reis, S. M. (1997). *The Schoolwide Enrichment Model: A how-to guide to educational excellence.* Mansfield, Conn.: Creative Learning Press.

Rosner, S. L., and Seymour, J. (1983). The gifted child with a learning disability: Clinical evidence. In L. H. Fox, L. Brody, and D. Tobin (eds.), *Learning-disabled/gifted children: Identification and programming* (p. 77–97). Baltimore, Md.: University Park.

Ruban, L. M. (2000). Patterns of self-regulated learning and academic achievement among university students with and without learning disabilities (doctoral dissertation, University of Connecticut, 2000). *Dissertation Abstracts International* (UMI No. TX 5–179–576).

Ruban, L. M., McCoach, D. B., McGuire, J. M., and Reis, S. M. (in press). The differential impact of self-regulatory methods on academic achievement among university students with and without learning disabilities. *Journal of Learning Disabilities.*

Schumaker, J. B., and Deshler, D. D. (1984). Setting demand variables: A major factor in program planning for the LD adolescent. *Topics in Language Disorders, 4*(2), 22–40.

Schunk, D. H., and Zimmerman, B. J. (eds.). (1994). *Self-regulation of learning and performance: Issues and educational implications* (pp. 75–99). Hillsdale, N.J.: Erlbaum.

Schunk, D. H., and Zimmerman, B. J. (eds.). (1998). *Self-regulated learning: From teaching to self-reflective practice.* New York: Guilford.

Silverman, L. K. (1989). Invisible gifts, invisible handicaps. *Roper Review, 12*(1), 37–42.

Shaw, S. F., Brinckerhoff, L. C., Kistler, J. K., and McGuire, J. M. (1991). Preparing students with learning disabilities for postsecondary education: Issues and future needs. *Learning Disabilities: A Multidisciplinary Journal, 2,* 21–26.

Sternberg, R. J. (1997). What does it mean to be smart? *Educational Leadership, 54,* 20–24.

Strauss, A. L., and Corbin, J. (1990). *Basics of qualitative research.* Newbury Park, Calif.: Sage Publications.

Tabachnick, B. G., and Fidell, L. S. (2001). *Using multivariate statistics* (4th ed.). Boston: Allyn & Bacon.

Tannebaum, A. J., and Baldwin, L. J. (1983). Giftedness and learning disability: A paradoxical combination. In L. H. Fox, L. Brody, and D. Tobin (eds.), *Learning disabled/gifted children* (pp. 11–36). Baltimore: University Park Press.

Tessler, L. (1997, September/October). How college students with learning disabilities can advocate for themselves. *LDA Newsbriefs.*

Vermetten, Y. J., Vermunt, J. D., and Lodewijks, H. G. (1999). A longitudinal perspective on learning strategies in higher education: Different viewpoints towards development. *British Journal of Educational Psychology, 69,* 221–242.

Vogel, S. (1997). *College students with learning disabilities: A handbook.* (Available from ADA bookstore, 4156 Library Road, Pittsburgh, PA, 15234, 412-341-1515.)

Vogel, S. A., and Adelman, P. B. (eds.). (1993). *Success for college students with learning disabilities.* New York: Springer-Verlag.

Vogel, S. A., and Reder, S. (1998). *Learning disabilities, literacy, and adult education.* Baltimore: Brookes.

Wang, M. C., and Palinsar, A. S. (1989). Teaching students to assume an active role in their learning. In M. C. Reynolds (ed.), *Knowledge base for the beginning teacher* (pp. 71–84). Elmsford, N.Y.: Pergamon.

Wehman, P. (1992). *Life beyond the classroom: Transition strategies for young people with disabilities.* Baltimore, Md.: Brookes.

Wells, S., and Hanebrink, S. (1998). Auxiliary aids, academic adjustments, and reasonable accommodations. In S. Scott, S. Wells, and S. Hanebrink (eds.), *Educating college students with disabilities: What academic and fieldwork educators need to know* (pp. 37–49). Bethesda, Md.: American Occupational Therapy Association.

Whitmore, J. (1980). *Giftedness, conflict, and underachievement.* Boston: Allyn & Bacon.

Whitmore, J. R., and Maker, J. (1985). *Intellectual giftedness in disabled persons.* Rockville, Md.: Aspen Publications.

Wilson, G. L. (1994). Self-advocacy skills. In C. A. Michaels (ed.), *Transition strategies for persons with learning disabilities* (pp. 153–184). San Diego, Calif.: Singular.

Wolters, C. A. (1998). Self-regulated learning and college students' regulation of their motivation. *Journal of Educational Psychology, 90*(2), 224–235.

Wong, B. Y., and Jones, W. (1992). Increasing metacomprehension in learning disabled and normally achieving students through self-questioning training. *Learning Disability Quarterly, 5,* 228–238.

Yost, D., Shaw, S., Cullen, J., and Bigai, S. (1994). Practices and attitudes of postsecondary LD service providers in North America. *Journal of Learning Disabilities, 27,* 631–640.

Zimmerman, B. J. (1989). A social cognitive view of self-regulated academic learning. *Journal of Educational Psychology, 81,* 329–339.

Zimmerman, B. J. (1990). Self-regulated academic learning and achievement: The emergence of a social cognitive perspective. *Educational Psychology Review, 2,* 173–201.

Zimmerman, B. J. (1998a). Academic studying and the development of personal skill: A self-regulatory perspective. *Educational Psychologist, 33*(2/3), 73–86.

Zimmerman, B. J. (1998b). Developing self-fulfilling cycles of academic regulation: An analysis of exemplary instructional models. In D. H. Schunk and B. J. Zimmerman (eds.), *Developing self-regulated learners: From teaching to self-reflective practice* (pp. 1–19). New York: Guilford Press.

Zimmerman, B. J., and Martinez-Pons, M. (1986). Development of a structured interview for assessing student use of self-regulated learning strategies. *American Educational Research Journal, 23,* 614–628.

Zimmerman, B. J., and Martinez-Pons, M. (1988). Construct validation of a strategy model of student self-regulated learning. *Journal of Educational Psychology, 80*(3), 284–290.

Zimmerman, B. J., and Martinez-Pons, M. (1990). Student differences in self-regulated learning: Relating grade, sex, and giftedness to self-efficacy and strategy use. *Journal of Educational Psychology, 82,* 51–59.

Zimmerman, B. J., and Paulsen, A. S. (1995). Self-monitoring during collegiate studying: An invaluable tool for academic self-regulation. In P. R. Pintrich (ed.), *Understanding self-regulated learning* (pp. 13–28). San Francisco: Jossey-Bass.

Zimmerman, B. J., and Schunk, D. H. (eds.). (1989). *Self-regulated learning and academic achievement: Theory, research, and practice.* New York: Springer-Verlag.

INDEX

A

Academic achievement, testing for, 9–10

Accommodations, 61–72; defined, 61–62, 80; elementary school, 64–65; high school, 69–72; middle school, 69–72

Acronyms, 167–196

Administration, 73–80; educational paperwork, 74; medical paperwork, 73–74; meetings, 75–76; special-services paperwork, 74

Administrative complaint process, 43–44

Age Eight Checklists, 257–258; developmental indicators checklist, 258; learning/cognitive disabilities checklist, 258; physical development checklist, 257; social/emotional disabilities checklist, 257

Age Five Disability Checklists, 249–251; developmental indicators checklist, 250–251; learning/cognitive disabilities checklist, 250; physical development checklist, 249; social/emotional disabilities checklist, 249

Age Four Disability Checklists: developmental indicators checklist, 247–248; learning/cognitive disabilities checklist, 247; physical development checklist, 246; social/emotional disabilities checklist, 246

Age Seven Checklists, 255–256; developmental indicators checklist, 256; learning/cognitive disabilities checklist, 256; physical development checklist, 255; social/emotional disabilities checklist, 255

Age Six Checklists, 252–254; developmental indicators checklist, 253–254; learning/cognitive disabilities checklist, 253; physical development checklist, 252; social/emotional disabilities checklist, 252

Age Three Disability Checklists, 243–245; developmental indicators checklist, 245; learning/cognitive disabilities checklist, 244; physical development checklist, 243; social/emotional disabilities checklist, 244

Americans with Disabilities Act, 78

Annual assessments, 95–97

Appropriate education rule, xiv–xv

Aptitude/cognitive ability, testing for, 9

Assessment: annual, 95–97, 120–121; daily, 95–96, 119–120; elementary school, 119–121; middle school, 139–141; observing your child's skills, 94–95; preschool to kindergarten, 95–97

Assignment sheets: elementary school modifications, 66–67; high school, 147; middle school, 70

Assistive technology, defined, 62, 80

Attendance sheet, 74

Autism, 5

B

Behavioral cues, and color, 103

Blending chart, 104–105

Blends activity, 104

Building-block skills, elementary school, 99–103; color, 100, 102; patterns/sequences, 100–101; sequencing, 101; visual cues, 101–103

Building-block skills, middle school, 124–139; assignment sheets, 125–126; day planner, 125; school schedule, 126–127; timers, 127

Building-block skills, preschool/kindergarten, 84–86; listening, 85–86; talking, 84–85

C

Capitalization, 112

Chunking, 107, 134

Cognitive development, 6

College, 160–161; compensation strategies, 157–159; documentation, 162–163; helping your child achieve success, 157–162; independence, encouraging, 159–160; motivation, 159; testing, 160–161

Color-coding, 147

Color skills, 100, 102

Combination plans, for inclusion, 53

Communication development, 6

Communication skills, preschool to kindergarten, 85–86

Community experience, and Statement of Intended Results, 151

Coordinated set of activities, 152

D

Daily assessments, 95–96

Daily living skills acquisition, and Statement of Intended Results, 151

Day planner, 125, 147

Deaf-blindness, 5

Desk calendar, 147

Developmental age, and educational products/toys, 58–59

Disability checklist s by age, 243–258; Age Eight Checklists, 257–258; Age Five Checklists, 249–251; Age Four Checklists, 246–248; Age Seven Checklists, 255–256; Age Six Checklists, 252–254; Age Three Checklists, 243–245

Due process, *See also* Procedural due process: appeals, 41–42; appearance at, 45; defined, 39; expectations for, 45–46; law suits, 42–43; lawyer, hiring, 46; negotiating, 44; paper trail, 45; procedures, 41; professionalism during, 44; and state education agency, 41–42

Due-process hearing: defined, 42; winning, 44–46

E

E-mail, 110

Early transition planning checklist, 153–154

Education of All Handicapped Students Act (Public Law 94–142), xiii

Educational environment, choosing, 57

Educational paperwork, 74

Educational products/toys, tips for buying, 57–59

Elementary school: accommodations, 64–65; assessment, 119–121; building-block skills, 99–103; lab room, 54–55; math skills, 113–118; meetings, 75; paperwork, 76–77; reading skills, 103–108; resource room, 54–55; self-contained classrooms, 55; special-education classrooms in, 53–54; special-needs classroom, 50; transitioning from middle school to, 123–124; writing skills, 108–113

Elementary school accommodations, 64–65; presentation, 64; responding, 64; setting, 65; timing, 64

Elementary school modifications, 65–69; assignments, 66–67; grading, 68; physical setting, 68–69; presentation, 65; setting, 66; testing adaptations, 67–68; timing, 66

Eligibility, determining, 3–15

Emotional development, 6

Emotional disturbance, 5

Employment, as life skill, 148

Employment/post-school living objectives, and Statement of Intended Results, 151

Environmental reading, 88–89

Environmental writing, 109–111

Evaluation Consent Form, 74

F

Financial management, as life skill, 148

Forms, 197–223

Free Appropriate Public Education (FAPE), 46

Functional vocational evaluation, and Statement of Intended Results, 151

G

General education classes, 54

H

Handwriting, 112–113

Healthcare, as life skill, 148

Hearing impairments, 5

High school: accommodations, 69–72; colleges, choosing for students with disabilities, 155–157; compensation strategies, 143–144; development and enrichment strategies, 146; inclusion in, 55–57; lab room, 56; life skills, 148; meetings, 76; paperwork, 77–78; resource room, 56; self-contained classrooms, 57; self-regulation, 144–147; social-emotional strategies, 146–147; special-needs classroom, 50–51; time-management skills, 147; transition planning, 154–155; transitioning to real world from, 149–155

Holiday cards, 110–111
Homework, middle school, 127–129
Housing, as life skill, 148

I

Idioms, 132–133
Independent educational evaluations (IEEs), 14
Individual Education Plan (IEP), xv, 15, 27–38;
    advocate role, 28–29; assistive technology and
    services:, 34; audiology, 34; counseling services,
    34; defined, 27; documentation, 77–78; early
    identification, 34; evaluation group, 31; family
    training, counseling, and home visits, 34; file clerk
    role, 29; health services, 34; implementation, 37;
    medical services, 34; nursing services, 34;
    nutrition services, 34; occupational therapy, 34;
    orientation and mobility services, 34; parent
    counseling and training, 34; physical therapy, 34;
    placement categories, 32–34; planning meeting,
    31–32; preparing to write, 29–30; private
    residential facility, 34; private separate facilities,
    33; procedural due process, 37; psychological
    services, 34; public residential facilities, 33; public
    separate facility, 33; recreation and therapeutic
    recreation, 34; reevaluations, 31–32; referrals to,
    27–28; rehabilitative counseling services, 34;
    sample form, 225–235; school health services, 34;
    service coordination services, 34; social
    work services in schools, 34; special-education
    outside the regular class, requirements for, 33;
    special education services, 27–29; special services,
    34–36; speech pathology/speech-language
    pathology, 34; team formation, 29–30; team
    member role, 28; transitioning to the individual
    Family Services Plan (IFSP), 25–26; transporta-
    tion and related costs, 34
Individual Family Services Plan (IFSP), 15, 17–26;
    Early Intervention services, 17–18, 20–21; forming
    a team, 21–22; information to supply at time of
    referral, 19; parents' responsibilities/role, 19–20;
    partnership, 18; planning meeting, preparing for,
    22–24; preparing to write, 21–24; referrals to,
    18–19; transitioning to the Individual Education
    Plan (IEP), 25–26; writing, 24–25
Individualized Family Service Plan (IFSP) (sample
    form #1), 197–215; child's present abilities/
    strengths, summary of, 202–204; cover, 197; family
    concerns/priorities/resources, 200–202; IFSP

outcomes, 205–207; IFSP Service Delivery Plan,
    208–210; IFSP Service review, 213–214; IFSP
    team, 198; important dates and events, 197–215;
    information, 198, 199–200; Parent/Coordinative
    Agency Agreement, 210–213
Individualized Family Service Plan (IFSP) (sample
    form #2), 215–223; "all about our child" section,
    217; "all about our family" section, 218; child's
    developmental status, 218; early intervention
    services, 221–222; family considerations, 216–217;
    family service planning team, 223; major outcomes,
    219; service settings/natural environment,
    220–221; Transition Planning Checklist, 222–223
Individualized Accommodation Plan (IAP), 3
Individuals with Disabilities Education Act (IDEA),
    xii–xiv; assistance stages, 12; basic requirements
    of, 4; categorical element of eligibility, 5–6;
    categories apply to children starting at age three,
    6; categories of disabilities for children 6-21, 5;
    defined, 3–4; disabilities, testing for, 8; eligibility,
    13–14; evaluating children ages 3-21, 11–13;
    evaluating children under 3, 10–11; functional
    element of eligibility, 6–8; independent educa-
    tional evaluations (IEEs), 14; learning disabilities,
    8–10; physical disabilities, 8; special-education
    teams, 13; transition planning, 150
Information processing, testing for, 9–10
Instruction, and Statement of Intended Results, 151
Interaction potential, and educational products/toys, 58
Internet resources, 259–263

J

Journals, 109–110

K

Kindergarten: assessment, 94–97; building-block
    skills, 84–86; math readiness, 91–93; reading
    readiness, 86–89; school tour, 83; special-needs
    tips, 83–87; writing readiness, 89–90
Knowledgeessentials.com, 40

L

Lab room: elementary school, 54–55; middle school
    and high school, 56
Late transition planning checklist, 154–155
Learning disabilities, 8–10
Least restrictive environment (LRE), xv, 34, 49, 51, 56,
    56–57, 151, 184

Letters, 110
Letters, and color, 102
Life skills, high school, 148
Linkages and responsible party(ies), 152
Listening skills, preschool to kindergarten, 85–86

M
Math readiness, 91–93; numbers activities, 91–92; one-to-one correspondence activities, 92–93; shape activities, 93
Math skills, elementary school, 113–118; clocks activity, 115; estimation activity, 115; grouping skills, 114; problem solving, 116–118; recommended supplies, 113–114; seasons activity, 115; timers activity, 114; weekly calendar activity, 115–116
Math skills, middle school, 136–139; calculations, 136–137; math language, 138–139; rules/procedures, 137–138
Media, and educational products/toys, 59
Medical paperwork, 73–74
Meeting invitation, 74
Mental retardation, 5
Middle school, 123–141; accommodations, 69–72; assessment, 139–141; building-block skills, 124–139; daily assessments, 140; homework, 127–129; inclusion in, 55–57; lab room, 56; math skills, 136–139; meetings, 76; paperwork, 77–78; reading skills, 129–133; resource room, 56; self-contained classrooms, 57; special-needs classroom, 50–51; time-management skills, 125–127; transition planning, 153–154; transitioning from elementary school to, 123–124; writing skills, 133–136
Middle school accommodations: assignments, 70; communication, 70; grading, 71; peer involvement, 71; physical setting, 71; presentation, 69; testing adaptations, 70
Middle school modifications, 71–72
Modifications, 61–72; defined, 62, 80; elementary school, 65–69; high school, 71–72; middle school, 71–72
Multiple disabilities, 5

N
Names, 87–88
No Child Left Behind Act (NCLB), xiii, 54
Nondiscriminatory evaluation rule, xiv

Notice of Proposed School District Action, 74
Notice of School District Refusal to Act, 74
Numbers, and color, 102

O
Odorn, Samuel L., 53
Opportunities for success, and educational products/toys, 58
Organizational skills, and color, 103
Orthopedic requirements, 5

P
Paperwork: elementary school, 76–77; high school, 77–78; middle school, 77–78
Parent participation, xvi
Patterns/sequences, 100–101
Physical development, 6
Physical disabilities, 8
Popularity, and educational products/toys, 59
Posting signs, 88–89
Postsecondary education, 163–166; choices, 166; planning for, 165–166; preparing for, 164
Power activity, 134–136
Prefixes/suffixes, 131–132
Preschool: accommodations, 63; assessment, 94–97; building-block skills, 84–86; inclusion in, 52–53; math readiness, 91–93; modifications, 63; reading readiness, 86–89; school tour, 83; special-needs classroom, 50; special-needs tips, 83–87; writing readiness, 89–90
Procedural due process, xvi, 37, 39–46, *See also* Due process; administrative complaint process, 43–44; conflict with child's school district, 40–41; defined, 39; law suits, 42–43; relief available, 43
Public preschool, inclusion in, 53

R
Reading readiness, 86–89; activities, 86–88; environmental reading, 88–89
Reading skills, elementary school, 103–108; blending chart, 104–105; blends activity, 104; chunking, 107; recommended supplies, 103; repeated reading, 107–108; word categories, 105–107
Reading skills, middle school, 129–133; idioms, 132–133; prefixes/suffixes, 131–132; student's bad attitude, 129–130; vocabulary, 131–133; your bad attitude, 130

Regular classroom: compared to special-needs classroom, 49–60; preschool, 52–53; when to include your child in, 51–57
Rehabilitation Act (Section 504), 78
Relationships, as life skill, 148
Repeated reading, 107–108
Resource room: elementary school, 54–55; middle school and high school, 56
Rhyming, 85–86

S
Schedule, 147
School subjects, and color, 102
School tour, 83
Scrapbooks, 110
Self-contained classrooms: elementary school, 55; middle school and high school, 57
Self-expression, and educational products/toys, 59
Sequencing, 101
Shopping, as life skill, 148
Signs, 88
Social development, 6
Special education, xiv, 4; defined, 27; identifying a child for, 27–28; types of disabilities qualifying or, 28
Special-needs classroom: inclusive setting, 49–50; middle school and high school, 50–51; preschool and elementary school, 50; regular classroom compared to, 49–60; special-education services, types of settings, 49–50; traditional setting, 49–50
Special services: exiting, 149–166; paperwork, 74
Speech or language impairments, 5
Statement of Intended Results, 151
Stories, 111
Structural skills, 111–112
Student participation, xvi

Substantive due process, defined, 39
Summary of Performance (SOP), 78–79; defined, 78; parts of, 79; student perspective, 80

T
Talking skills, preschool to kindergarten, 84–85
Thank-you notes, 110
Time-management skills: high school, 147; middle school, 125–127
Transition plan, paperwork, 78
Transition planning, 150, 153–155
Traumatic brain injury, 5

V
Vision statement, 150–151
Visual cues, 101–103
Visual impairments, 5
Vocabulary, 131–133
Vocational Rehabilitation Act (1973), xii
Vocational Rehabilitation Comprehensive Assessment process, 78

W
Word categories, 105–107
Writing readiness: activities, 89–90; fine motor skills, 89–90; writing letters, 90
Writing skills, elementary school, 108–113; capitalization, 112; e-mail, 110; environmental writing, 109–111; handwriting, 112–113; holiday cards, 110–111; journals, 109–110; letters, 110; scrapbooks, 110; stories, 111; structural skills, 111–112; thank-you notes, 110
Writing skills, middle school, 133–136; activities, 133–136; chunking, 134; power, 134–136

Z
Zero reject rule, xiv

The Knowledge Essentials Series

Everything You Need to Know to Help Your Child Learn, Grades PreK – 4

Amy James

Preschool: 978-0-471-74814-4
Kindergarten: 978-0-471-74813-7
First Grade: 978-0-471-46818-9

Second Grade: 978-0-471-46820-2
Third Grade: 978-0-471-46821-9
Fourth Grade: 978-0-471-46819-6

The key to your child's educational success is in your hands

"Knowledge Essentials is a remarkable series that will benefit children of all abilities and learning styles … I highly recommend it for all parents who want to make a difference in their children's education." —**Michael Gurian**, author, *The Minds of Boys*

"Finally, a book about teaching young children by somebody who knows her stuff!" —**LouAnne Johnson**, author, *Dangerous Minds* and *Teaching Outside the Box*

"Having examined state standards nationwide, Amy James has created innovative and unique games and exercises to help children absorb what they *have* to learn, in ways that will help them *want* to learn. Individualized to the child's own learning style, this is a must-have series for parents who want to maximize their child's ability to succeed in and out of the classroom." —**Myrna B. Shure, Ph.D,** author of *Thinking Parent, Thinking Child*

The Knowledge Essentials series enables parents to work alongside their child's teachers and take an active role in their child's education. Each book explains to parents what their child is learning at a particular grade level and what educational standards to expect in the subjects of math, language arts, science, and social studies. The many activities provided in each book, easily adaptable to different learning styles, show parents how to take effective steps to strengthen any weaknesses and supplement what happens in the classroom. With these books, parents will be able to pinpoint their child's learning style, monitor his or her progress in school, and help their child meet his or her full academic potential.

Amy James, a former social studies teacher, is a nationally respected authority on educational compliance issues and the No Child Left Behind Act. Her company, Six Things, Inc., provides consulting services for national media, publishers, and school districts on compliance with state and national education standards, as well as professional development for K–12 teachers.